PENGUIN BOOKS

SHAKESPEARE'S PROBLEM PLAYS

E. M. W. Tillyard, Litt.D., who was Master of Jesus College, Cambridge, from 1945 to 1959, and a university lecturer in English for nearly thirty years, ranked among the leading authorities on both Shakespeare and Milton. He was born in 1889 and attended a school in Lausanne and the Perse School, Cambridge, before proceeding to Jesus College, where he gained a Double First in Classics and was Craven Student. After studying archaeology in Athens, he returned as a fellow to Jesus College in 1913. He was on active service in France and at Salonika during the First World War, at the end of which he was a liaison officer with the Greek forces. His publications include *Milton*, *Shakespeare's Last Plays*, *Shakespeare's History Plays*, *The Miltonic Setting*, *The Elizabethan World Picture*, *Shakespeare's Problem Plays*, *The Metaphysicals and Milton*, and *The Epic Strain in the English Novel*. Dr Tillyard, who was married and had three children, died in 1962.

SHAKESPEARE'S PROBLEM PLAYS

E. M. W. TILLYARD

PENGUIN BOOKS
IN ASSOCIATION WITH CHATTO & WINDUS

PENGUIN BOOKS

Published by the Penguin Group
Penguin Books Ltd, 27 Wrights Lane, London W8 5TZ, England
Penguin Books USA Inc., 375 Hudson Street, New York, New York 10014, USA
Penguin Books Australia Ltd, Ringwood, Victoria, Australia
Penguin Books Canada Ltd, 10 Alcorn Avenue, Toronto, Ontario, Canada M4V 3B2
Penguin Books (NZ) Ltd, 182–190 Wairau Road, Auckland 10, New Zealand

Penguin Books Ltd, Registered Offices: Harmondsworth, Middlesex, England

First published by Chatto & Windus 1950
Published in Peregrine Books 1965
Reprinted in the Penguin Shakespeare Library 1970
Reprinted in Pelican Books 1985
Reprinted in Penguin Books 1993
1 3 5 7 9 10 8 6 4 2

Copyright 1950 by E. M. W. Tillyard
All rights reserved

Printed in England by Clays Ltd, St Ives plc
Set in Monotype Bembo

CONTENTS

PREFACE

THIS study of four of Shakespeare's plays was written for delivery as the Alexander Lectures at the University of Toronto for the academic year 1948–9. Professor W. J. Alexander, who died in 1944, held the chair of English at University College, Toronto, from 1889 to 1926, and the lectureship was founded as a tribute to his distinction as teacher and scholar. The first series was delivered in 1929–30.

I wish to thank the Toronto authorities for honouring me by their invitation to give these lectures, and I am particularly grateful to Professor A. S. P. Woodhouse for his kindness and help in arranging the details of their delivery.

No student of Shakespeare's Problem Plays can fail to be indebted to W. W. Lawrence's *Shakespeare's Problem Comedies* (New York, 1931). This book not only tells us things about these plays which we did not know or did not heed before, but by its vigour and charm induces us to read them with fresh eyes. As usual I have got much profit and stimulus from the relevant portions of Mark Van Doren's *Shakespeare* (New York, 1939), even when I disagree (as I do immoderately over the style of *Troilus and Cressida,* for instance). The brief critical remarks in Peter Alexander's *Shakespeare's Life and Art* (London, 1939) have made me think and have helped me greatly. A memorable lecture by Hardin Craig on Shakespeare's bad poetry, delivered at Stratford on Avon in August 1947 and printed in the first volume of *Shakespeare Survey* (Cambridge, 1948) has given me courage and authority to speak boldly on certain topics about which I might have been timid. For associating *Hamlet* with the three plays I mainly treat, and not with *Othello* and the other later tragedies, I can invoke the precedent of F. S. Boas in his *Shakespeare and his Predecessors*. It is but too easy to take E. K. Chambers's *William Shakespeare* (Oxford, 1930) quite for granted: a kind of institution, used but not talked of. I make the effort not to take it for granted, and I record my debt to its constant utility.

Other debts will be acknowledged in the notes at the end of the different chapters.

E. M. W. T.

NOTE TO THE
PENGUIN SHAKESPEARE LIBRARY EDITION

Some suggestions for further reading on the plays treated in this volume (excluding *Hamlet*) are to be found in the Pelican edition (1985) of W. W. Lawrence's *Shakespeare's Problem Comedies*.

INTRODUCTION

THE three plays I originally set out to discuss, *Troilus and Cressida*, *All's Well That Ends Well*, and *Measure for Measure*, have been called 'dark comedies' and 'problem comedies', while the first has been called a 'satirical comedy'. Though not fond of any of these names, I recognize that the plays make a group and that a common name is needed. As a choice of evils 'problem comedies' gives least offence. But, finding, however reluctantly, that *Hamlet* goes with these plays (or at any rate with *Troilus and Cressida*) more aptly than with the three undoubted tragedies usually grouped with it, I cannot use 'problem comedies' for all four plays; and 'problem plays' is the only available term.

It is anything but a satisfactory term, and I wish I knew a better. All I can do now is to warn the reader that I use it vaguely and equivocally; as a matter of convenience. The warning is the more necessary because 'problem play' can mean something reasonably definite. L. J. Potts in his forthcoming book on comedy says of the problem play that it 'treats the situations that arise in society simply as moral or political problems, in the abstract and without reference to the idiosyncrasies of human nature', and he cites *Everyman*, *Troilus and Cressida*, and the plays of Galsworthy. This is a good definition, but for my present purposes too good and too precise; for though it may include *Troilus and Cressida* it does not extend to *All's Well*. To achieve the necessary elasticity and inclusiveness, consider the connotations of the parallel term 'problem child'.

There are at least two kinds of problem child: first the genuinely abnormal child, whom no efforts will ever bring back to normality; and second the child who is interesting and complex rather than abnormal: apt indeed to be a problem for parents and teachers but destined to fulfilment in the larger scope of adult life. Now *All's Well* and *Measure for Measure* are like the first problem child: there is something radically schizophrenic about them. *Hamlet* and *Troilus and Cressida* are like the second problem child, full of interest and complexity but divided within themselves only in the eyes of those who have misjudged them. To put the difference in another way, *Hamlet* and *Troilus and Cressida* are problem plays because they deal with and display interesting problems; *All's Well* and *Measure for Measure* because they *are* problems.

In sum, the term problem play can have a wide meaning, and if in using it I have to be equivocal I had rather be so than not use it at all.

One large matter I had better mention at once and get rid of summarily. Many readers have found in the Problem Plays a spirit of gloom, disillusion, and morbidity that exceeds dramatic propriety and demands some extrinsic explanation in Shakespeare's private life at the time. Others on the contrary think that such readers have unconsciously begun from Shakespeare's supposed biography and have insisted on reading that biography into this group of plays. Between these two extremes there may be many intermediate positions. I need not be concerned with them in these lectures. The whole matter has been thoroughly aired, and all I need do is to take sides. And I take it with those who think such personal explanations superfluous, or at least too uncertain to be worth anything. I agree here with Sisson* on the

* C. J. Sisson, *The Mythical Sorrows of Shakespeare*, British Academy Shakespeare Lecture for 1934.

mythical sorrows of Shakespeare and with R. W. Chambers* in his prefatory remarks on *Measure for Measure* concerning the early years of James I, and the small need Shakespeare had to be unhappy just then, or with this sentence of W. W. Lawrence:

Critics have, I think, been too much inclined to emphasize one or more possible explanations of the peculiar characteristics of the problem comedies – personal misfortune or bereavement, disappointment in friendship or in love, the degeneration of the age, the demands of the theatre, the influence of prevailing literary and dramatic fashions, haste and carelessness, and so forth.

However, though it may be vain to conjecture from external evidence how Shakespeare's emotions were behaving at this period, we can infer from the plays themselves that he was especially interested in certain matters. Some of these occur in all the plays, some in at least three; and, when pointed out, they will serve to make a genuine group of the four plays which so far I have separated into two pairs.

First, Shakespeare is concerned throughout with either religious dogma or abstract speculation or both. It may be retorted that so he was also when he wrote his later tragedies. Yet there is a difference, in that dogma and speculation are less completely absorbed into the general substance of the Problem Plays; they are felt rather more for their own and rather less for the drama's sake, as if, in this form at least, they were new and urgent in Shakespeare's mind, demanding at this point statement and articulation rather than solution and absorption into other material. Hamlet is powerfully aware of the baffling human predicament between the angels and the beasts, between the glory of having been made in God's image and the incrimination of being descended from fallen Adam. Gertrude in re-marrying in haste appeared to him worse than a beast wanting discourse of reason. Again, if man was the glory of the world he might still be aghast

* R. W. Chambers, *The Jacobean Shakespeare and Measure for Measure,* British Academy Shakespeare Lecture for 1937.

at being allowed to crawl between heaven and earth. In *All's Well* the wretched insufficiency of natural man is pointed to at a most emphatic place in the play (IV. 3. 24).

> *A:* Now, God lay our rebellion! as we are
> ourselves, what things are we!
> *B:* Merely our own traitors.

When in *Measure for Measure* Isabella speaks of the atonement,

> Why, all the souls that were were forfeit once;
> And he that might the vantage best have took
> Found out the remedy,

she is indeed speaking in character, and the doctrine has been quite assimilated into the dramatic context; but there is so much theological lore elsewhere in the play on the relation of Justice and Mercy (and less assimilated into the dramatic context) that we need not doubt that the doctrine of the forfeit soul was present in Shakespeare's own mind at that time. In *Troilus and Cressida* there is little or no theology but abundance of speculation, for instance on the question whether worship can be only of a worthy object or whether it can invest the object with a worthiness not its own.

Other instances must wait till I treat the separate plays, but I believe the above to be fair samples and to show Shakespeare in a mood of uncommon abstraction and speculation.

Thoughtfulness about man's estate and about religious dogma must be serious to be worth anything but it need not be pessimistic. And the mood of these plays is serious but not black. In *Hamlet* Shakespeare glories in his sense of the wonder and the diversity of life, which though it can be terrible is not bad. There is much satire in *Troilus and Cressida*; but the play is not fundamentally satirical, implying that things can, not must, go like that. By far the most melancholy of the four plays is *All's Well*, but not because Shakespeare treats his subject cynically.

Certainly Helena is too sombre and Bertram too unpleasant to be heroine and hero of normal comedy; but neither character is satirized. They are realistic, and Shakespeare was interested in the detailed workings of their minds. The play is unusual, difficult to label, but not pessimistic. On the other hand the pervading melancholy suggests that Shakespeare was tired when he wrote and that he forced himself to write. In *Measure for Measure* the themes of mercy and forgiveness are treated in all sincerity with no shadow of satire. There is much good and much evil presented in the play; but no hint that evil is the rule. Any failure it argues in Shakespeare is not of morale but of technique. The plays then are powerfully united by a serious tone amounting at times to sombreness; they show a strong awareness of evil, without being predominantly pessimistic.

I mentioned the realistic characterization of Helena and Bertram; and this exemplifies a second large quality of the Problem Plays: an acute interest in observing and recording the details of human nature. Such an interest exists of course through the whole series of Shakespeare's plays, but in very different ways and degrees. In the early History Plays the realism peeps out fitfully in the minor characters, like Cade's followers, but it is there just as surely as anywhere else. In the last plays, though held in absolute control, it is often subordinated to the symbolic presentation of characters, as in the statue scene in the *Winter's Tale*. Now in the Problem Plays Shakespeare was interested in observing and recording the details of human nature for its own sake in a way not found elsewhere. It is as if at that time he was freshly struck by the fascination of the human spectacle as a spectacle and that he was more content than at other times merely to record his observation without subordinating it to a great overriding theme. The beginning of this fresh interest may perhaps be seen in *Henry IV*. If so, it is suspended in *Julius Caesar*. But certainly by the time of *Othello* observation, though acute and brilliant, is held in strict subordination. In the interim Hamlet, Troilus, Bertram, and Angelo are all of them characters embodying their author's powerful interest and pleasure in the varieties and the possibilities of the human mind.

It is these two interests – in speculative thought and in the working of the human mind – pursued largely for their own sake that partly characterize the Problem Plays. And from them spring characteristic virtues and defects. They create a peculiar sense of real life but they prevent the sharp clarity of intention we are apt to demand of very great art. There is no need to follow this topic here, since I shall resume it in dealing with the separate plays.

So much for general matters: I pass to some details which the plays have in common. In each play, but in different degrees of importance, recurs the theme 'a young man gets a shock'. Hamlet, indeed, has just got his first shock when the action opens, and before long he gets another. The two shocks motivate the whole play. Claudio has just had a shock when the action of *Measure for Measure* opens, but though it sets much of the action in motion it is not a principal part, for other themes, arising indeed from it, usurp the interest. In *Troilus and Cressida* and *All's Well* Troilus and Bertram get first a smaller and then a greater shock in the course of the action. Troilus's first shock is to be separated from Cressida, his second is to witness her infidelity. Bertram's first shock is to be forcibly married, his second is to undergo a long series of surprises and alarms on the night before he leaves Florence to return to France. Shakespeare must have been specially interested at this time in different types of young men on the verge of manhood and in the harsh experiences that force them to grow up. If *Measure for Measure*, as is usually thought, is the latest, it looks as if this interest had begun to work itself out by then, for Claudio and his development are drawn but slightly. All the same we are led to think that Claudio *does* grow up. When (IV. 2. 69) the Provost shows him his death-warrant and asks where is Bernardine, he says,

14

As fast lock'd up in sleep as guiltless labour
When it lies starkly in the traveller's bones.
He will not wake.

This cool and reflective reply shows him a different man from the hasty and unreflective lover of Juliet. So the full theme does recur in *Measure for Measure*, even if not very emphatically.

If Claudio is slightly drawn, the other three young men are drawn in great detail. Bertram and Troilus belong to what Lafeu calls 'the unbaked and doughy youth of a nation'; and it may well be that Pandarus's long moral about 'tarrying the leavening, and the kneading etc.' in the first scene of *Troilus and Cressida* is meant to apply not only to the process of winning Cressida but to the process of growing up. Hamlet is anything but 'unbaked and doughy' in the sense that Bertram is; yet he has an emotional tenderness and a sensitive idealism that belong to adolescence and which are forcibly brought to maturity in the course of the play. Here then is a master-motive, and one that binds the four plays strongly together.

Secondly, in at least three of the plays, the business that most promotes this process of growth is transacted at night. There are so many night-scenes in Shakespeare that such an observation may amount to little. Yet the repetition is so striking that I find it difficult to believe it fortuitous. I do not mean any conscious plan, but instinctively Shakespeare staged the most critical phase of growth in darkness. If Hamlet develops at all in the play, it is principally during the night when the *Murder of Gonzago* was acted and when, having killed Polonius, he spoke out to his mother. It is in the depth of the night that Troilus, witnessing Cressida's infidelity, has years of mental growth imposed on him in a brief hour. Bertram's last night at Florence is crowded with disturbing happenings: the receipt of a severe letter from his mother; news of his wife's supposed death which upsets his equanimity over his supposed seduction of Diana; the unmasking of the man on whom he relied, Parolles. The effect of all these happenings is not disclosed till the end of the play, but we cannot doubt it. In *Measure for Measure* the case is different. There indeed the night-scene occurs, and in the corresponding place. But there is no sense of the darkness synchronizing with a change in Claudio's mind. On the contrary we picture him as resigned soon after Isabella has repudiated his plea for his life. The one touch of full analogy comes when Angelo soliloquizes after midnight on his supposed seduction of Isabella:

> This deed unshapes me quite, makes me unpregnant
> And dull to all proceedings. A deflower'd maid,
> And by an eminent body that enforc'd
> The law against it!

Here are some tokens of remorse and at least the chance of mental change. And Angelo, though not adolescent in years, was in some ways immature.

There is a deep propriety in these midnight crises. It is not only that thought and the dark go together, as in *Il Penseroso*, but that we naturally conceive the most significant growth to take place unseen and in silence: notions to which the darkness and stillness of night correspond.

Thirdly (and allied possibly to Shakespeare's interest in adolescence) is his interest in the old and new generations and in old and new habits of thought. It appears only in *Troilus and Cressida* and *All's Well*, but doing so in that pair and not in one of the two common pairs it is likely to represent a genuine interest belonging to the whole period. It is not new for it was very evident in Shakespeare's second historical tetralogy. There, the antique medieval world of Richard II is set side by side with the newer world of Henry IV. The same sort of contrast exists in the Trojans and Greeks in *Troilus and Cressida*. The Trojans are antique, anachronistically chivalrous, and rather inefficient; the Greeks are the new men, ruthless and, though quarrelsome and unpleasant, less inefficient than the Trojans. In *All's Well* the contrast is between age and youth. The castle at Rossillion and the court at Paris are controlled by pathetic relics of a gracious past. To these relics the new generation is sharply contrasted. It has energy and strong will, but graciousness and elegance are not among its virtues. It looks as if Shakespeare were aware at this time of the social and economic changes that were taking place. In his last plays he came to picture the new generation differently.

The matters, largely of plot and structure, common to *All's Well* and *Measure for Measure*, are too obvious to need special mention. The two plays hang together much as do *Cymbeline*, the *Winter's Tale*, and the *Tempest*. But it is worth noting that the way these two plays convey a moral norm differs from that of *Hamlet* and *Troilus and Cressida*. *All's Well* and *Measure for Measure* abound in moral statements. In the first the two French Lords and in the second Escalus and the Provost form the *punctum indifferens* in their respective plays. *Troilus and Cressida* is different. There the morality is not conveyed through any one person or set of persons. It is rather choric and to be gathered from what a number of people say when they are least themselves and most rhetorical mouthpieces. Ulysses is not a highly moral character himself; but his great speeches, choruslike, convey the principle of order which is essential for judging the play's emotional turbulence. The case is rather the same in *Hamlet*. Horatio is not strong enough to be the moral *punctum indifferens* in his own right. But there is a lot of choric morality as well.

Such are some of the common characteristics of the group. I have stated them briefly and dogmatically, postponing amplification or proof to my treatment of the separate plays.

Much has been added in recent years to our knowledge of Shakespeare's thought, of his imagery, and of his contemporary setting; and it should all be to the good. The danger is that it should blind us to the poetic logic of the actual text. For instance, in learning that a certain type of image occurs frequently in a play we may easily forget that frequency, a mere numerical thing, may mean little compared with poetic emphasis: that a certain type of image occurring once but in a poetically emphatic place may have more weight than another type that occurs ten times in less emphatic places. We need in fact a weighing-machine like that pictured in the *Frogs* of Aristophanes for the contest between Aeschylus and Euripides. But such a machine is imaginary, and the only substitute is the reader's apprehension of the total poetic effect.

Some of the criticism of the Problem Plays seems to me to incur the above danger by abstracting the thought too crudely from its dramatic context. It may not be for me to criticize, since I have probably done the same in writing of Shakespeare's History Plays. But for my present treatment I have tried to follow the poetic and not the mere abstracted significances and to allow the poetic or dramatic effect to dictate the relative emphasis. How far I have succeeded can only appear in my treatment of the plays themselves.

HAMLET

SINCE *Hamlet* is usually classed as a tragedy, I recognize my obligation to explain why I go against habit and class it as a problem play. Where you class it will depend on your notion of tragedy; so I must begin by stating my own.

No single formula will cover all those works we agree to call tragic: at least three types of feeling or situation are included in the word. The first and simplest is that of mere suffering; and it has been very well set forth by J. S. Smart.* Suffering becomes tragic when it befalls a strong (even a momentarily strong) nature, who is not merely passive but reacts against calamity. Then 'There is a sense of wonder', and the tragic victim

contrasts the present, weighed as it is with unforeseen disaster and sorrow, with the past which has been torn from him: it seems as if the past alone had a right to exist, and the present were in some way unreal. . . . The stricken individual marvels why his lot should be so different from that of others; what is his position among men; and what is the position of man in the universe.

This simple conception is needed because it includes certain things which we recognize as tragic but which elude any conception more rigid or more complicated. The *Trojan Women* and the *Duchess of Malfi* are tragedies of simple suffering, where the sufferers are not greatly to blame. In fact the conception resembles the simple medieval one, with the addition that the

* *Essays and Studies of the English Association*, VIII, 26.

sufferer's quality of mind causes him to protest and to reflect. *Hamlet* is certainly, among other things, a tragedy of this kind. Terrible things do befall its protagonist; while as a tragic hero Hamlet lacks a complication and an enrichment common in much tragedy: that of being to some extent, even a tiny extent, responsible for his misfortunes. Othello and Samson were partly responsible for theirs. Even with Desdemona and her loss of the handkerchief we think faintly that perhaps she was the kind of person who might have been so careless. No one could accuse Hamlet of being the kind of person whose mother was bound to enter into a hasty and incestuous re-marriage, of being such a prig that his mother *must* give him a shock at any cost. If you read the play with a main eye to the soliloquies, you can easily persuade yourself that *Hamlet* is principally a tragedy of this first simple kind.

The second type of tragic feeling has to do with sacrificial purgation and it is rooted in religion. The necessary parties in a sacrifice are a god, a victim, a killer, and an audience; and the aim is to rid the social organism of a taint. The audience will be most moved as the victim is or represents one of themselves. The victim may be good or bad. Shakespeare's Richard III is a perfect example of a sacrificial victim carrying the burden of his country's sins; and he is bad. Once again, *Hamlet* is tragic, and in this second way. There is something rotten in the state of Denmark, and one of its citizens, blameless hitherto and a distinguished member of society, is mysteriously called upon to be the victim by whose agency the rottenness is cut away. And when Hamlet curses the spite by which he was born to be the victim and the cure, we thrill because it might be any of us. Like the first we can make this second tragic feeling the principal thing, if we narrow our vision sufficiently. But we should be wrong, for in actual fact our sense of Denmark's rottenness is much weaker than our sense of what a lot happens there. Denmark is not at all like Macbeth's Scotland, for instance, where the social and political theme is dominant. We have the liveliest sense of Malcolm destined to rule a purged body politic; no one gives a thought to Denmark as ruled by Fortinbras.

A third kind of tragic feeling has to do with renewal consequent on destruction.* It occurs when there is an enlightenment and through this the assurance of a new state of being. This kind penetrates deep into our nature because it expresses not merely the tragedy of abnormal suffering but a fundamental tragic fact of all human life: namely that a good state cannot stay such but must be changed, even partially destroyed, if a succeeding good is to be engendered. This paradox of the human condition, however plain and unescapable, is hard to accept: nevertheless tragedy gives us pleasure in setting it forth and making us accept it. The usual dramatic means of fulfilling this tragic function is through a change in the mind of the hero. His normal world has been upset, but some enlightenment has dawned, and through it, however faintly, a new order of things. Milton's Samson is for a second time reconciled to God, and this second reconciliation is other than the earlier state of friendship with God, which was destroyed. Othello is more than the stoical victim of great misfortune. He has been enlightened and though he cannot live it is a different man who dies. Those tragedies which we feel most centrally tragic contain, with other tragic conceptions, this third one. It is partly through failing to contain this conception that *Hamlet* is separated from the three great tragedies with which it is popularly joined. But this is a contentious statement which must be substantiated.

The main point at issue is whether Hamlet's mind undergoes during the course of the play a revolution comparable to that which takes place in the minds of Oedipus, or Lear, or Samson. If it does not, there can be no question of tragedy in the third sense. Till recently this point was hardly at issue, and my last paragraph would not have contradicted the general assumption.

* See M. Bodkin, *Archetypal Patterns in Poetry* (London, 1934), sections I and II, for this topic, psychologically elaborated.

But a fundamental change in Hamlet's mind has since been very confidently asserted. For instance, Middleton Murry sees a clear progress in the play ending with the hero's regeneration. The key-soliloquy ('To be or not to be . . .') states the master-theme, Hamlet's terror of death, and

> it is in the main in his conquering his fear of the unknown futurity that Hamlet's victory lies. That is the central line of his progress and his growth. He has to teach himself, as it were all over again, to make a mouth at the invisible event.*

He has to learn to be brave with his whole mind, and not only when he momentarily forgets himself. He becomes wholly brave when just before the fencing-match he 'defies augury' and immediately afterwards apologizes to Laertes 'with the simplicity and candour of a reborn soul'. C. S. Lewis speaks of *Hamlet* largely in terms of a state of mind, the state of thinking about being dead, but he too finds the same progress in the mind of the hero:

> The world of *Hamlet* is a world where one has lost one's way. The Prince also has no doubt lost his, and we can tell the precise moment at which he finds it again. 'Not a whit. We defy augury. There's a special providence in the fall of a sparrow. . . .'†

Both writers rely for their opinions mainly on a single passage, the prose conversation between Hamlet and Horatio in v. 2 after Osric has gone out bearing with him Hamlet's acceptance of an immediate fencing-match with Laertes. They think this passage (containing Hamlet's 'defiance of augury') marks the revolution in Hamlet's mind. If they are wrong here, their argument cannot hold. Here, therefore, it is crucial to make a decision. It is one that can be made only through our own response as we read.

* J. Middleton Murry, *Shakespeare* (London, 1936), p. 248.

† *Hamlet, the Prince or the Poem*, British Academy Shakespeare Lecture for 1942, p. 13.

Amleth, Belleforest, the First Quarto, and *Der bestrafte Brudermord* are here irrelevant.

As I read it the passage shows no fundamental change in Hamlet's mind;* and for two main reasons.

First, any piety shown here by him was anticipated earlier in the play. He has been from the first remote from natural, unregenerate man. He is deeply religious, as the complete man of the Renaissance ought to be. And the signs of his piety and his belief that 'the readiness is all' in other and earlier parts of the play argue that in the present passage he exhibits no spiritual development. When Horatio tries to restrain him from following the Ghost with 'Be ruled: you shall not go', Hamlet replies 'My fate cries out'. What better example of 'the readiness is all' turned to action? And he had already protested that the Ghost could do nothing to his soul, 'being a thing immortal as itself'. His sense of the glory of man as created in God's image ('What a piece of work is a man!') and of his ignominy as a fallen creature ('Virtue cannot so inoculate our old stock but we shall relish of it') is theologically impeccable. And his words on Polonius's dead body are equally so:

> For this same lord
> I do repent: but heaven hath pleased it so,
> To punish me with this and this with me,
> That I must be their scourge and minister.
> I will bestow him and will answer well
> The death I gave him.

Nothing in the 'defiance of augury' speech is more pious and regenerate than this. Hamlet did not change.

But a more important reason is the tone of the passage. And this is not new and profound and significant, but elegantly conventional. Quietism not religious enlightenment is the dominant note. Hamlet is ready for anything that will come along; he has not acquired a new and liberating mastery of his own fate.

* For a more detailed discussion see Appendix A, p. 142.

If therefore this crucial passage shows nothing new, the notions of a regenerate Hamlet, and hence of a play tragic in the fullest sense, are ruled out. Further, even though *Hamlet* is tragic in certain senses, that tragic quality is not the principal quality. If it is not the principal quality (and I do not deny its importance as an ingredient) it remains to say what those principal qualities are.

To lead up to these, I will first correct a possible false impression. In denying to Hamlet any powerful spiritual growth, any definitive spiritual revolution, I may have given the impression that his mind was quite static. This I did not intend; for the religious is not the only type of mental growth, and it is possible that Hamlet without undergoing a religious regeneration does change in some sort. Indeed it would be strange if all the things Hamlet had to suffer made no impression on his mind. Thus Theodore Spencer argues* that Hamlet's soliloquies show a progress in his power to convert the personal into the general, and that in the end he is above rather than in the tumult. This, I believe, is to argue from single passages in abstraction from the play. And even if Hamlet's soliloquies do show a progression from the personal, his behaviour at Ophelia's funeral, which comes after all the soliloquies, shows a very thorough relapse. On the other hand, the notion that Hamlet grows older during the play is surely true. Not that we should be dogmatic about Hamlet's precise age. V. Østerburg† has argued very sensibly that the fixing of his age at thirty on the authority of the Grave-Digger is to ignore the Elizabethan habit of speaking in round numbers that were never meant to be precise. But Shakespeare does succeed in making us picture Hamlet as an older man by Act Five, just as he did Troilus. Hamlet wrestling with Laertes in Ophelia's grave is indeed not above the tumult but he is older than his undergraduate self at the beginning. All the same such an ageing is no more than an impression appropriate to all that

* *Shakespeare and the Nature of Man* (New York, 1942), p. 108.
† *Prince Hamlet's Age* (Copenhagen, 1924).

Hamlet has endured. It is not an independent theme, and the things that Hamlet endures are more important than the changes in himself that his endurance brings about.

On the other hand, though the things Hamlet endures may not work a spiritual revolution in him they do have their effect on the given ingredients of his mind. And that effect has its own order. Again, this order is not the principal thing in *Hamlet* but it has high importance. To speak of this importance is useless till I have made out a case for the order itself. In so doing I shall have to be highly subjective, for the order will depend less on what is stated than on the ways in which the poetic stress appears to the reader to fall. Further, to be at all brief, I shall have to be dogmatic on just those matters which have been the subject of most doubt and controversy: namely on what passes on Hamlet's mind; for what gives the order I seek to elucidate is the degree of prominence different events assume in Hamlet's mind and any action he takes to meet them.

First, I must recall Granville-Barker's timely and emphatic reminder* that the accepted act divisions are misleading and that the play falls naturally into three parts. The first corresponds with the first act and ends with Hamlet's acceptance of the task given him by the Ghost. The second begins with Polonius sending Reynaldo to Paris (II. 1) and ends with Hamlet's departure to England (IV. 4). The last begins with Ophelia's madness (IV. 5) and comprises the rest of the play. Between the parts there are long lapses of time. The first part presents Hamlet's state of mind, the position he is in, and the problems of action involved; the second presents the action and counter-action of Hamlet and Claudius; the third presents the consequences of what happened in the second.

Next, I must record my agreement with Waldock in the great prominence he gives to Hamlet's first soliloquy 'O that this too too solid flesh would melt' and in his surprise that from Goethe

* H. Granville-Barker, *Hamlet* (London, 1937), p. 34.

and Coleridge (and one might now add from Middleton Murry and C. S. Lewis) one would not gather that before the coming of the Ghost anything had happened to trouble Hamlet. Of the import of the soliloquy Waldock writes:

> A terrific calamity has befallen Hamlet, his whole nature is upturned. And the particular origin of his trouble is made perfectly plain. It is the recent re-marriage (indecently hasty and incestuous re-marriage) of his mother. This event has changed the whole of life for him, the realization of all that it seems to imply is poisoning his very soul.*

The truth of these remarks is so obvious that one can only marvel at the great need that undoubtedly existed and still exists for making them. The impression the shock left is conveyed later in Hamlet's bitter words to his mother in the third act, but the nature of the shock itself can best be understood by Troilus's words when he has ocular proof of Cressida's infidelity:

> This she? no, this is Diomed's Cressida:
> If beauty have a soul, this is not she;
> If souls guide vows, if vows be sanctimonies,
> If sanctimony be the gods' delight,
> If there be rule in unity itself,
> This is not she. O madness of discourse,
> That cause sets up with and against itself!
> Bi-fold authority, where reason can revolt
> Without perdition, and loss assume all reason
> Without revolt; this is and is not Cressid.
> Within my soul there doth conduce a fight
> Of this strange nature that a thing inseparate
> Divides more wider than the sky and earth,
> And yet the spacious breadth of this division
> Admits no orifex for a point as subtle
> As Ariachne's broken woof to enter.
> Instance, O instance, strong as Pluto's gates:
> Cressid is mine, tied with the bonds of heaven,

* A. J. A. Waldock, *Hamlet* (Cambridge, 1931), p. 15.

Instance, O instance, strong as heaven itself:
The bonds of heaven are slipp'd, dissolv'd, and loos'd;
And with another knot, five-finger-tied,
The fractions of her faith, orts of her love,
The fragments, scraps, the bits and greasy relics
Of her o'er-eaten faith, are bound to Diomed.

(V. 2. 137)

Such, we may infer, was the kind of shock Hamlet received. It was a fact that his mother would hang on his father as if increase of appetite had grown by what it fed on; and it was another fact that within a month she had married his uncle. And the two facts, of which he had utter personal evidence, could not be reconciled. When such a shock is recounted in the earliest place in the play where Hamlet is able to reveal himself, that is his soliloquy in the second scene, we may surely expect that the rest of the play will deal largely with the working out of this shock. It should also be observed that in his soliloquy Hamlet says nothing about his uncle having cheated him of the succession; he thinks only of his mother's action, which has made the world ugly for him, and (in a lesser degree) of his uncle's unworthiness.

In the next scene – that is before Hamlet meets his father's ghost – we hear of his courtship of Ophelia; and I think the critics have been backward in seeing the great prominence of this motive, which occurs so early in the play and at the very time when the themes that are to prevail are being set forth. The chief value of Clutton-Brock's little book on *Hamlet* lies in his perception that Hamlet is unkind to Ophelia because he sees in her a repetition of his mother; but I believe we may go farther and say that the way Act One is organized suggests that Hamlet's very first advances to Ophelia had to do with his mother's second marriage. He hoped to find in Ophelia evidence to contradict what his mother's action appeared to prove. Not that we are justified in working out a time-table for *Hamlet* (after the manner of those appendices of Bradley that read like a parody of the text

of *Shakespearean Tragedy*); but the order of dramatic presentation
bids us connect Gertrude and Ophelia closely and to expect that
Polonius's orders to Ophelia to deny her presence to Hamlet will
have a powerful bearing on the course of the play. By the end of
the third scene therefore the overwhelmingly important theme is
Gertrude's re-marriage, its effect on Hamlet reinforced by
Ophelia's behaviour, and the probability of further consequences.
Nor, if this theme was to count during the course of the play,
could Shakespeare have spared making it so prominent in view of
the force of the next two scenes, when Hamlet meets his father's
ghost. Well, the Ghost commands Hamlet to avenge his murder
and, though putting an end to the incestuous connection of
Claudius and Gertrude, not to contrive anything against his
mother:

> Let not the royal bed of Denmark be
> A couch for luxury and damned incest.
> But, howsoever thou pursuest this act,
> Taint not thy mind; nor let thy soul contrive
> Against thy mother aught. Leave her to heaven
> And to those thorns that in her bosom lodge
> To prick and sting her.

The words are ambiguous. It is not clear whether in upbraiding
his mother as Hamlet later did he was transgressing his father's
command. But at least the Ghost couples what are by now
evidently the master-themes, the vengeance on Claudius and the
lascivious and incestuous guilt of Gertrude. And it is the co-
existence of the two themes and the contrasted ways in which
Hamlet responds to them that give the play what regularity of
structure it possesses. It must not be forgotten that the first act
closes with the Ghost scene; and not only by modern editorial
conjecture. Though there are no act divisions in the Quartos,
there are in the Folio up to the end of Act Two, and it is good that
the Folio confirms the obvious pause in the action, implying that
the main themes have now been stated, at this point.

The second act, which begins the true second part, develops both themes without bringing them to a crisis. Hamlet's disgust at his mother had prompted his dealings with Ophelia; and her actions in their turn exacerbate his feelings against her, his mother, and all women. Hamlet's experience with his father's ghost had dealt a second shock to his mind, bringing with it the danger of derangement and prompting him to assume a fictitious derangement in addition and to express the conflict in his feelings through long soliloquies. This derangement alarms Claudius and causes him to take precautions. The next act contains Hamlet's answers to the two shocks he has suffered in the first act; and they consist of his testing the Ghost's veracity through the play, followed by his sparing Claudius immediately after, and of his upbraiding his mother. There is no interval between his dealing with Claudius and his dealing with his mother, and these should be considered jointly yet in contrast; so considered, they match the manner in which the two themes had been set forth in the first act. Interpretations of the play-scene, of the sparing of Claudius,* and of Hamlet's words to his mother vary and will continue to vary; but such variety will not affect the plea that the scenes must be considered together in correspondence with the master-motives as set forth in the first act, and that thus they give the play a recognizable shape. My impression is that Hamlet forces himself in his dealings with Claudius, lashing himself to hysteria but not acting with his whole heart, while he puts his whole self into his words to his mother. In the deepest sense, therefore, he disobeys the Ghost's commands. Hamlet's brutal words to Ophelia in the play-scene tell the same tale, for they show him thinking of his mother's action and of his disgust of womankind at the very crisis of his dealings with Claudius. While, then, in the two scenes that mainly concern Claudius Hamlet shows himself histrionic, artificially self-excited, and even hysterical, in talking to his mother he shows the full range of his character and relieves his

* For a note on Hamlet's motives see Appendix B, p. 144.

long-suppressed feelings by speaking from his heart. Moreover in his positive advice to her he finds an outlet for the active side of his nature. This is the supreme scene of the play. Psychologically, what resolution there is in the play is mainly here. Once Hamlet can face his mother and share with her the burden of what he thinks of her, he can at least begin to see the world as something other than a prison. In the very act of rating his mother he does a justice to Ophelia which the bleeding body of Polonius ironically renders incapable of any happy consequence. Hamlet calls his mother's re-marriage

> such an act
> That blurs the grace and blush of modesty,
> Calls virtue hypocrite, takes off the rose
> From the fair forehead of an innocent love,
> And sets a blister there.

He is of course thinking of Ophelia, of her true innocence and of his own treatment of her as if she were a harlot. (How, by the way, do those who consider Hamlet's coarseness to Ophelia as an undigested relic from the old play get around these lines? Surely if Shakespeare himself gives an explanation, it is idle to seek further.) It is in this scene too that Hamlet, although terrified by the Ghost, overwhelmingly vehement in denunciating the loathsomeness of his mother's sexual sin, and callous over the body of Polonius ('I'll lug the guts into the neighbour room'), shows his most winning sanity and the utmost delicacy of his sensibilities. When, on the Ghost's exit, he protests that his pulse keeps time as temperately as his mother's, the words that follow bear his protest out. What better could illustrate his sane and delicate and critical temper than the sudden interpolation into his preaching to his mother of

> Forgive me this my virtue,
> For in the fatness of these pursy times
> Virtue itself of vice must pardon beg,
> Yea, curb and woo for leave to do him good.

His final callousness over Polonius's body did not exclude his pious words quoted earlier about his deed, while his final disposition towards his mother is tender. All these exhibitions, even if they are fragmentary, of sanity and clean feeling come after Hamlet has relieved his mind of his horror at his mother's act; and, coming also after and in spite of the Ghost's interposition urging revenge, are surely meant to show us that his mother's act rather than the obligation to his dead father usurps the main part of his mind. What we learn from this most revealing scene is that Hamlet (unlike the world at large) does not really believe that it is relevant to kill Claudius: that will not bring his father back to life. To awaken Gertrude's sense of guilt is his fundamental need.

Hamlet's conversation with his mother does not cure him, does not altogether rescue him from his prison, but it does either initiate a slow healing process or render him less impatient of his burdens. His bad conscience about the revenge stirs again, on his way to take ship to England, in his last soliloquy ('How all occasions . . .'). Later, on his return, he exhibits violent passions at Ophelia's funeral. Yet these relapses do not efface the sense of Hamlet's having obtained a real relief and being more resigned. And this more resigned temper persists till the end of the play. In the third part (from Hamlet's return from England) the psychological interest, from the preponderant motives of Hamlet's mind having been revealed, shifts partly to the other characters and now counts for less compared with the interest of the plot; the details of which evolve with perfect propriety from the events recounted in the second part.

Hamlet, then, does possess a shape. The states of mind presented in the first act lead to certain actions in the second act and are tested and clarified in the third. Thus clarified they persist to the end of the play. This shape contributes substantially to the poetic quality; and mainly on the intellectual side, giving the sense of a masterly controlling brain. But psychological explication showing intellectual mastery, and spiritual action are not the same. At most Hamlet regains some of the dignity and composure that we know to have been part of his original endowment. Out of the wreck of his affection and respect for his mother something may have been salved. By comparing what has been regained or salved with what formerly existed whole we do indeed get a pleasant sense of order. But, with no great revelation or reversal of direction or regeneration, the play cannot answer to one of our expectations from the highest tragedy.

This failure does not mean that *Hamlet* is not one of the greatest plays. On the contrary, the subtlety and the fascination of its psychological appeal (within the limits indicated) joined with the simple but firm lines of its general shaping exalt it to eminence.

Even so I do not place these matters, however important, quite among the principal things, and it remains to say which these are.

The first is the sheer wealth and vigour and brilliance of all the things that happen. In fact one of *Hamlet*'s virtues resembles that of Masefield's *Odtaa*, where the sheer variety and the very lack of a rigorous type of causal logic for every detail are part of the point. In addition to the general shaping I have been at pains to describe, there are more casual sequences of detail, comparable to the way one word may suggest another. *Man – monkey – monkeypuzzle – difficulties of climbing – Alps – Swiss francs*: the sequence of thought is obvious enough. But it is a superficial sequence by means of only one out of numberless details comprised in each item. Yet its very casualness is related to life and is not alien to art. The entry of the Players in *Hamlet* is perfectly contrived and linked: yet it has just that casual character. Simply as a play of things happening, of one event being bred out of another, and of each event being described with appropriate and unwearied brilliance, *Hamlet* is supreme. Such an opinion can claim the support of Horatio, who in almost the last words of the play describes the action as having consisted

> Of carnal, bloody, and unnatural acts,
> Of accidental judgements, casual slaughters,
> Of deaths put on by cunning and forced cause,
> And, in this upshot, purposes mistook
> Fall'n on the inventors' heads.

The effect of all these events so masterly presented is primarily one of vitality. One is tempted to call *Hamlet* the greatest display of sheer imaginative vitality in literary form that a man has so far achieved. It is here we feel that Shakespeare first reached the full extent of his powers; and he gives us the sense of glorying in them. And no other play of Shakespeare gives us just that touch of sheer exultation.

The second principal matter has to do as much with the setting as with the business of the play. To explain it I will proceed indirectly. Aristotle said that poetry answered two profound human instincts: those of imitation and of harmony or rhythm. The first had to do with the desire to learn. It matters less what Aristotle in this highly compressed passage of the *Poetics* precisely meant than that he suggested a distinction of fundamental importance. Thoughtful people are puzzled by the appearance life presents to them. Their hour-to-hour experiences do not satisfy them and are felt to convey a false impression. The impression is both impoverished and unordered, and they wish to have it enlarged and interpreted. In fulfilling this wish people will do the work for themselves or obtain help from others in proportions that accord with their capacities. The great artists do a great deal of the work for themselves and offer a great deal of help to others. The help they offer will be through enrichment and through ordering or interpretation, corresponding to Aristotle's distinction between imitation and harmony or rhythm. The artists by the richness of their presentation enlarge the range of experience comprehensible by the unaided efforts of the ordinary person, and by the form of their presentation suggest some order in this range of experience. A great artist will excel in both functions. But, however great he is, he has to compromise and to adjust the scope of one function to that of the other. If he is very great, he will wish to present a variety of such compromises, for each type of compromise will express something that none of the others can.

To apply the above to Shakespeare's tragedies. *King Lear* is the play where the balance is most evenly struck. In *Othello* the content of experience is less and the emphasis falls more on the ordering. *Hamlet* is best understood as a play less of ordering than of sheer explication or presentation, as a play presenting the utmost variety of human experience in the largest possible cosmic setting.

It is strange that a play so dominated as it would seem by one character should convey so rich a sense of varied humanity and human activity. But this is what happens, and criticism has erred in treating the profundities and the paradoxes and the turnings of Hamlet's mind as the substance of the play rather than as the means of expressing another substance. It is not the interest and variety of Hamlet's mind that comes first but the wonder and variety of all human experience which his quality of mind makes peculiarly evident; just as to a psychologist lunatics are chiefly interesting not in themselves but because by isolating and exaggerating an ordinary mental proclivity they make its workings clearer and hence give new information about the workings of the ordinary mind. Hamlet, the achieved Renaissance young man of the most varied accomplishment, is in his normal self well equipped to reflect an abundant human experience: subjected to two shocks that come near to upsetting his reason, his capacities are enlarged still further and his sensibilities so worked on, that experience as now reflected in him takes on a new and terrifying intensity. Nor must we forget the abundance of humanity and of human action that reinforces the range of Hamlet's mind in suggesting multifarious existence. It is not only of minor characters such as Osric that I am thinking, but of such passages as Marcellus's description in the first scene of the preparations for war. Unnecessarily particularized for the requirements of the plot, it somehow forces one to hear the beat of hammers in the distance as the accompaniment of the scene and to bear in our minds the notion of ordinary physical life going on behind the heightened passions of the main actors.

Critics have spoken of the difficult or intractable material Shakespeare inherited from his traditional story. Difficult it may have been, but in the end perfect for his purposes. Aiming not at tidiness or homogeneity or a classical shape, he could use the antique barbaric nature of his material to contrast as sharply as possible with the modern refinement and sophistication of his hero. Moreover it is a contrast true in a double sense: in the familiar sense that refinement and civilization are but a thin crust on a much greater mass of barbarism and disorder; and in the sense that Shakespeare's own England was a violent blend of the crude and the delicate.

Shakespeare's picture of the varieties of human experience was of course conditioned by the contemporary world picture. And I doubt if in any other play of Shakespeare there is so strong an impression of the total range of creation from the angels to the beasts. Maybe in the *Tempest* the lower stretches of the chain of being and the doubtful stretches between man and angel are more fully presented, but the angels and man's variety in his own great stretch of the chain are presented there with less emphasis. This way of looking at creation is powerfully traditional and Christian; and in *Hamlet* if anywhere in Shakespeare we notice the genealogy from the Miracle Plays with their setting of Heaven, Purgatory, and Hell, as for instance in the hero's description of himself as a fellow 'crawling between heaven and earth'. Indeed, one of the best analogies with the total landscape of *Hamlet* is Langland's description of the fair field full of folk at the opening of *Piers Plowman*. *Hamlet* is one of the most medieval as well as one of the most acutely modern of Shakespeare's plays. And though the theme of spiritual regeneration may be absent from the plot, the setting includes the religious consciousness most eminently.* But lest this medievalism remain too little qualified, let me give a second analogy: with Homer's description of the scenes on the shield of Achilles. It is a brief description, dealing mainly with ordinary life and aimed at correcting the more narrowly martial trend of the *Iliad* as a whole, but it includes the picture of the ocean and the stars, and blended with the variegated adventures in the body of the poem, sets forth Homer's surpassing awareness of the wonder and diversity of life and of the fateful conditions under which it is transacted.

I hope that the bearing of my last pages on the question whether *Hamlet* is a tragedy or a problem play has been apparent. I will end by speaking explicitly on this topic. The tragic mode is ideally very definite and formal. Motives are clear in the characters, and the spectator has no doubt where his sympathies should lie. We know that Medea has been hardly treated and also that she acted with deplorable violence. We know that Macbeth was a villain in having Banquo murdered. Further, in ideal tragedy life is presented in a startlingly clear and unmistakable shape: we are meant to see it indubitably so and not otherwise. When sheer explication, or abundance of things presented, takes first place, then we leave the realm of tragedy for that of the problem play. Here it is the problems themselves, their richness, their interest, and their diversity, and not their solution or significant arrangement, that come first. I have argued that *Hamlet*, though containing tragedy of sorts, and though reinforced intellectually by a noble general shape, belongs principally to this type. The same is true of *Troilus and Cressida*, though it has less tragic content. And to this play I turn next.

* For the contention that in *Hamlet* Shakespeare shows himself the heir of Christian Platonism see Joseph E. Baker, *The Philosophy of Hamlet*, in the Parrott Presentation Volume (Princeton, 1935), pp. 455–70.

Notes on *Hamlet*

No one is likely to accept another man's reading of *Hamlet*. Of the three weighty books that have been published in recent years on the course of the play's action (J. Dover Wilson, *What Happens in 'Hamlet'*, Cambridge, 1935; H. Granville-Barker, *Hamlet*, London, 1937; L. L. Schücking, *The Meaning of Hamlet*, London, 1937) I have found the second most congenial, though I differ completely on the matter of Hamlet's regeneration, in which Granville-Barker agrees with Middleton Murry and C. S. Lewis. More especially I have found Granville-Barker very helpful in his sections on the shaping of the plot. But I have found the best interpretation of the action of *Hamlet* in Dowden's footnotes to his edition in the Arden Shakespeare. Dowden read the text very closely and with sensitive sympathy, and his notes are better criticism than his section on *Hamlet* in *Shakspere, his Mind and Art*. This is not surprising, because Dowden's *Hamlet*, first published in 1899, is twenty-four years later than his *Shakspere*.

A. J. A. Waldock's *Hamlet* (Cambridge, 1931) has helped me in various ways, particularly in its encouragement not to miss the play for the critics. I agree with the respect he accords to A. C. Bradley's treatment of the play.

Though I cannot read *Hamlet* generally in the way G. Wilson Knight does (*The Wheel of Fire*, London, 1930), I agree with his insistence on the fundamental irrelevance to Hamlet of killing Claudius: 'What would have been the use of killing Claudius? Would that have saved his mother's honour?' (p. 33).

TROILUS AND CRESSIDA

ALTHOUGH the contemporary setting cannot ensure an answer to the main questions that *Troilus and Cressida* insists on posing it can help tell us the kind of play it is and, even more, is not. In Victorian times many readers refused to give it a proper chance because they thought it degraded the high Homeric treatment of the Trojan War. Today the case is different: there are fewer readers of Homer, and of these a smaller proportion would insist on the sanctity of the Homeric tradition. Besides, the recent findings of scholarship that Shakespeare's Trojan War is medieval and not classical are beginning to penetrate the consciousness of the non-academic reader. A recent attempt to answer the main questions through associating *Troilus and Cressida* with a type of play, satirical comedy, which then enjoyed a brief vogue, does not succeed, but it does help to explain why Shakespeare chose a form that was neither tragedy, comedy, nor history through which to say the things he wished to say.

It is usual, in glossing Shakespeare's treatment of the Trojan War, to say that this war had long ceased to be heroic, that to the medieval reader the Greeks had always been the enemy and an ill-natured set, and that as time went on the Trojans too were tarnished; further, Cressida during the fifteenth and sixteenth centuries became proverbial as a wanton and a lazar, so that Shakespeare could not possibly have made her the character Chaucer made her, and finally Shakespeare's un-Homeric and apparently cynical treatment of his material was quite to be expected in view of the state in which the material reached him. Such a general conception is useful in warning us what not to expect, but I believe that Shakespeare's medieval predecessors can help us rather more than is usually allowed.

First, it is well to understand that *Troilus and Cressida* need bear no relation to those books of Chapman's Homer published in 1598. It is true that Shakespeare was very unlikely not to have read them, but it is equally true that the bulk of his material was medieval and that for the small residue he need not have gone to Chapman. Homer had long been known in Latin and was hence accessible to many readers, and the way he treated the war must have been common knowledge. There was no need of Chapman's translation to tell the Elizabethans that Thersites was a railer – Erasmus, among others, had made that clear long ago. And Shakespeare's Thersites himself, though exclusively Homeric in origin, is un-Homeric in function; he is a version of the Elizabethan Fool, and hence a privileged person. When in the second book of the *Iliad* Odysseus hits Thersites on the back with his golden staff for railing at King Agamemnon and raises a bloody weal, all the Greek leaders laugh sweetly. But Shakespeare's Achilles defends Thersites from Ajax, who had no business to hit a licensed fool for sharp words. The other matter that is at least partly Homeric and not medieval is the duel between Hector and Ajax. It is true that there was one – and a very important one – in the *Troy Book*, but it was an accidental one in a battle. The challenge, Nestor's complaint that the Greek chieftains are slack in accepting the challenge, the choice of the Greek defendant by lot, and the breaking off of the duel by heralds are all absent from the *Troy Book* and come from Homer. But even so Shakespeare makes the whole episode a very medieval affair conducted according to the rules of chivalry. Remotest of all from Homer is Hector's protest that

> He hath a lady, wiser, fairer, truer,
> Than ever Greek did compass in his arms.

The insistence on the close kinship of Hector and Ajax is also medieval. Shakespeare *may* have got some of the non-medieval details of the duel from Chapman's *Iliad* but he could have got them from Homer direct, through his small Greek, or from a Latin translation, or from hearsay. Had he taken Chapman very seriously he must have motivated Achilles's sloth as Homer does in his first book, through his anger at being bereft of Briseis. But he does not: he first lets us think that Achilles is merely proud and moody and later brings in the medieval motive, his love for Polyxena. No, we should think of Chapman only by the way and rather pay our attention to the great inherited conception of Troy as the rich and wonderful city whose fall was one of the most striking and exemplary achievements of Time and during whose flourishing so many chivalric or base or romantic deeds were transacted. Shakespeare himself had made poetry of these conceptions years before in the *Rape of Lucrece*. First, in her protest against Time and Opportunity, Lucrece describes it as Time's glory to calm contending kings, to ruinate proud buildings and smear with dust their glittering golden towers, and to feed oblivion with decay of things. This is very much the same Time, which in *Troilus and Cressida* is the arbitrator of the Trojan War, which dusts over the gilt of past deeds, and which feeds that great-sized monster, Oblivion, with their fragments. Later, Lucrece, meditating on her own sacrifice to Opportunity and Time, thinks of another ruin of Time, the city of Troy, and she describes episodes from the siege, recollecting them from a painting. Sinon, the traitor and proverbial as such in the Middle Ages, is dwelt on, for he corresponds to Tarquin. Lucrece does not find the extreme of misery

> Till she despairing Hecuba beheld
> Staring on Priam's wounds with her old eyes,
> Which bleeding under Pyrrhus' proud foot lies.

>In her the painter had anatomized
>Time's ruin. (1447-51)

If these lines look forward to *Hamlet*, the rest of the descriptions
show that the elements of the Trojan world of *Troilus and Cressida*
existed in Shakespeare's mind many years before. First, there is
the guilt of Helen and Paris, the criminal weakness of Priam, and
the tragedy that society should suffer for the private quarrels of a
few. The passage deserves quoting in full, if only to show that
Shakespeare could speak bitterly of war at a time when, according to the rules, he ought to have been feeding on the elation of
the post-Armada years, untouched by the disillusion later ex-
perienced through the history of Essex. Lucrece exclaims:

>Show me the strumpet that began this stir,
>That with my nails her beauty I may tear.
>Thy heat of lust, fond Paris, did incur
>This load of wrath that burning Troy doth bear:
>Thy eye kindled the fire that burneth here;
>And here in Troy, for trespass of thine eye,
>The sire the son the dame and daughter die.
>
>Why should the private pleasure of some one
>Become the public plague of many moe?
>Let sin, alone committed, light alone
>Upon his head that hath transgressed so;
>Let guiltless souls be freed from guilty woe:
>For one's offence why should so many fall,
>To plague a private sin in general?
>
>Lo, here weeps Hecuba, here Priam dies,
>Here manly Hector faints, here Troilus swounds,
>Here friend by friend in bloody channel lies,
>And friend to friend gives unadvised wounds,
>And one man's lust these many lives confounds.
>Had doting Priam check'd his son's desire,
>Troy had been bright with fame and not with fire.
>
>(1471-91)

Note how Hector and Troilus are mentioned together, the two Trojan heroes, against the Homeric treatment. The other characters mentioned are Achilles, Nestor, Ajax, and Ulysses. Achilles bears no character, but the other three are as they were later to be in *Troilus and Cressida*:

> In Ajax' eyes blunt rage and rigour roll'd,
> But the mild glance that sly Ulysses lent
> Show'd deep regard and smiling government.

> There pleading might you see grave Nestor stand
> . . . his beard, all silver white,
> Wagg'd up and down.   (1398–1401, 1405–6)

Precisely whence Shakespeare derived his notions of Troy we cannot know. Many may have reached him through conversation. But the kind of tradition he was open to is shown neatly enough in a poem he may or may not have read, Hawes's *Pastime of Pleasure*. The penultimate chapter is on Time and his acts. And one of his chief acts was the destruction of Troy – and no other fallen city is mentioned:

> Do not I, Tyme, cause nature to augment,
> Do not I, Tyme, cause nature to decay,
> Do not I, Tyme, cause man to be presente,
> Do not I, Tyme, take his lyfe away,
> Do not I, Tyme, cause death take his say,
> Do not I, Tyme, passe his youth and age,
> Do not I, Tyme, every thynge asswage?

> In tyme Troye the cyte was edyfied;
> By tyme also was the destruccyon.

And casually, in the eighth stanza of the twentieth chapter comes the mention of Priam's folly in allowing the war to happen at all.

> The myghty Pryant, somtyme kynge of Troye,
> Wyth all his cyte so well fortyfyed,
> Lytle regarded all his welth and joye,

Wythout wysdome truely exemplyfied,
His propre death him selfe he nutrifyed;
Agaynst his warre wysdome did reply,
At his grete nede to resist the contrary.

Troy fell, one of the supreme works of Time, and it was the Trojans' fault, even if they were better knights than the Greeks.

In his preface Hawes mentions his 'maister Lydgate, the monke of Bury, floure of eloquence'; and there is no doubt that Lydgate was one of the writers most responsible for spreading the traditions about Troy of which I have been speaking. But before I come to Lydgate's picture of the Trojan War, I must ask the question how Shakespeare is likely to have read and heeded him.

It is generally admitted that Shakespeare drew from both the main English works deriving from Guido delle Colonne's prose version of the Troy legends, Lydgate's *Troy Book* and Caxton's *Recuyell of the Histories of Troye*. I believe one may go farther and say that he went to Caxton for some of his facts but that he found Lydgate much more useful in suggesting ideas and motivation. For instance, though both mention the six gates of Troy, and in the same order, it is from Caxton that Shakespeare in his prologue takes the forms of the names 'Dardan and Timbria, Helias, Chetas, Troien, And Antenorides'. But take the scenes in Lydgate and Caxton where Ulysses, Nestor, and Diomed try to persuade Achilles to fight, scenes which correspond to Ulysses's conversation with Achilles in *Troilus and Cressida*, III. 3, and you will find that there is nothing in Caxton that resembles Shakespeare except possibly Achilles's protest that 'in the end there is no prowess but it be forgotten', while these lines of Lydgate dwelling on the need to keep renown fresh are close in sentiment though not in poetic force to Ulysses's 'Time hath, my lord . . .'. Ulysses appeals to Achilles

By youre manhood, that is spoke of so ferre
That your renoun to the worldis ende
Reported be, whereso that men wende,

Perpetually, by freshnes of hewe
Day by day to encrese newe,
That the triumphe of this highe victorie
Be put in story and eke in memorie,
And so enprented that foryetilnes
No power have by malis to oppresse
Youre fame in knyghthod, dirken or difface,
That shyneth yit so clere in many place
Withoute eclipsynge, sothly this no les;
Which to conserve ye be now rekeles
Of wilfulnes to cloude so the lyght
Of youre renoun that whilom shon so bright,
Youre mighy hond of manhood to withdrawe.

(IV. 1770–85)

There are of course places where the debt is doubtful. Achilles kills Hector in *Troilus and Cressida* as he kills Troilus in Lydgate and Caxton; and there is no doubt that Shakespeare draws from one or the other, or from both simultaneously. But we cannot be certain which alternative to choose. Such a detail matters little compared with the general and pervasive influences. And the probability here may be settled by picturing how Shakespeare was likely to have come across his originals. Such inquiries are unusual; but it may really make a difference to know not only what his most influential original was likely to be but also whether he had acquired his material in the past, meditated on it and recollected it, or whether he came on it suddenly and for the first time and cast it into dramatic form while still fresh in his mind. It is plain from *Lucrece* that he had long known the medieval matter of Troy, and it is highly probable that he knew it primarily from Lydgate.

After having superseded Chaucer as the most popular English poet in the late fifteenth and early sixteenth centuries Lydgate gradually dwindled from that high position but became firmly established as one of the few early English classics. Right at the end of the sixteenth century and shortly before Shakespeare wrote *Troilus and Cressida* Meres wrote that 'England hath three ancient poets, Chaucer, Gower, and Lydgate'. Nashe in his preface to Greene's *Menaphon* (1589) mentions Chaucer, Lydgate, and Gower as ancient English poets to set up against the Italians. Three years earlier Webbe's *Of English Poetry*, in its survey of English poetical production, began with Gower and Chaucer, and went on to Lydgate and *Piers Plowman*, adding that there was nothing else to note till the reign of Henry VIII. The most popular of all poems in Shakespeare's boyhood, the *Mirror for Magistrates*, professed to continue Lydgate's *Fall of Princes*. It could never have done so unless Lydgate had been a much read poet. I have no doubt myself that Shakespeare read Lydgate as a youth, along with the other early writers or works enumerated, just as I believe he read Hall's *Chronicle*. There is no proof, and yet the probability is overwhelming unless we make Shakespeare a freak among poets. Boys and youths who feel the true urge to versify want to know what the poets of contemporary reputation have written, and habitually satisfy that want by voracious reading. Far from cramming up Gower in middle age in order to compose the choruses of *Pericles* Shakespeare must have read him in his youth as one of the English classics, venerable if quaint. And we shall never get *Troilus and Cressida* right unless we think of a Shakespeare steeped as a youth in the antique and venerable and quaint world of Lydgate's Troy.

This is not a popular supposition, for the notion of an unread Shakespeare, whose first stirrings of mind came from contact with the stage, is still widely prevalent in England. In his edition of *Macbeth*** (1947) Dover Wilson doubts whether Shakespeare ever looked into the *Mirror for Magistrates*, unless to read Sackville's contributions. I can only be amazed at such a sentiment. The *Mirror* was so popular in Shakespeare's youth that edition followed edition with new 'tragedies' often added. Even with a

* In the New Cambridge Shakespeare, p. xliv, note 3.

45

lukewarm taste for poetry Shakespeare could hardly have kept aloof. It may be that in America, where so much work has been done on the conditions in which he must have grown up, the notion of Shakespeare in his youth reading what was then thought to constitute the English poetical classics will not appear improbable.

What would Shakespeare have found in Lydgate's *Troy Book* and in a more factual and less moralized form in Caxton's *Recuyell*? First of all a world antique yet familiar, rather ridiculous but still, as literature, useful; a version of the world of medieval chivalry. The city that Priam built on the ruins of the old city of Laomedon surpassed in glory anything actually on earth. Priam himself was a peerless king, tall, bold, just, musical, incorruptible, an early diner, and above all a cherisher of worthy knights. His sons too were peerless. Hector was the first knight in the world, the spring and well of knighthood, the ground, root, and crop of chivalry. Paris was the handsomest man and the best archer in the world. Troilus, it is true, could not be peerless because of Hector, but he was nearly as formidable. Polyxena (in spite of Helen) was peerless, and when Nature created her she put forth a unique effort to make her excel all other women in beauty and in morals. In scope Lydgate is lavish. The tale of Troy as we think of it extending from the rape of Helen to the sack of the city is preceded by the story of how Laomedon's city was destroyed by Hercules (with the adventures of the Argonauts included) and is followed by the adventures of the Greek chieftains up to the death of Ulysses. Romantic excess prevails in the Trojan War proper. Hector twice kills a thousand Greeks single-handed in one battle. When Hector has been killed, Troilus takes his place as the first Trojan hero and performs similar prodigies. Fighting on the Trojan side was a monstrous archer (or sagittary). He was man down to his middle and horse below, but he neighed like a horse. He had a fiery face and flaming breath; and he did great execution among the Greeks until Diomed killed him.

But Lydgate, as well as transmitting this romantic material, is its critic. He is a courageous and original moralist. In a most prominent place, near the beginning of Book Two which opens the main Trojan War, he condemns that war and many others too as springing from a trivial cause.

> We trewly may adverten in oure thought
> That for the valu of a thing of nought
> Mortal causes and werris first by-gonne;
> Strif and debate here under the sonne
> Wer meved first of smal occasioun
> That caused after gret confusioun,
> That no man can the harmys half endite.
> For, for a cause dere y-nowghe a myte
> Eche is redy to distroien other;
> A man for litel will strive with his brother:
> Blood is unkynde, whiche gretly is to drede.
> Allas, whi nyl thei taken better hede?
> For olde Troye and afterward the newe
> Thorughe smal enchesoun, who the trothe knewe,
> Wer finally brought to distruccioun.
>
> (II. 123–37)

For all Priam's many virtues Lydgate blames him sharply for being responsible for the war. After Priam had rebuilt Troy he lived in peace and prosperity until envy stirred him to avenge the detention of Hesione by the Greeks. It was malice that

> Made him wery to lyven in tranquille
> And mevid him, of his iniquite,
> Upon the Grekis avenged for to be.   (II. 1084–6)

And it was Priam who stirred up his sons to vengeance. Through the mouth of Cassandra Lydgate insists on the sin of abducting Helen and the punishment Troy will get from it:

> O wrechid Troye, errying in this cas
> Withinne thi silfe to suffre this trespas,

> For to concent unto swyche folye
> In sustenyng of foule avoutrye
> That Paris shulde takye unto wyve
> The quene Elyne whos husband is alyve.
>
> (II. 4195–200)

And as well as saying that the war offends the sanctity of marriage, she reiterates the Trojans' folly in having stirred up trouble when they were prosperous. Nor is Hector himself blameless, for his death was due to his sin of covetousness. Seeing a Greek knight wearing jewelled armour, he forgets prudence in coveting this armour. He kills the knight, and the better to strip him puts his shield on his back. This gives Achilles the chance of a treacherous attack. Lydgate reprimands Hector severely:

> Desyre of havynge, in a gredy thought,
> To highe noblesse sothly longeth nought,
> Nor swiche pelfre, spoillynge, nor robberie
> Apartene to worthi chivalrye;
> For covetyse and knyghthod, as I lere,
> In o cheyne may not be knet y-fere.
>
> (III. 5361–6)

Not only that, but Hector was culpably negligent in not accepting the gifts of fortune. In the first great battle after the Greeks established the bridgehead the Trojans were victorious. Hector killed Patroclus and carried the battle into the Greek ships. Then he had a duel with his kinsman Ajax, who persuaded him for friendship sake to call off the day's battle. Hector imprudently yielded, and fortune's favours were over for good. Caxton, for once, is as strong a moralist as Lydgate when he describes this episode, though he bases his criticism more solely on the folly of refusing fortune's favour and does not put it in terms of mistaken chivalry. Here is his piece of moralizing:

The unhappy Hector accorded to him his request and blew an horn and made all his people to withdraw into the city. Then had the Trojans begun to put fire in the ships of the Greeks and had all brent them, ne had Hector called them fro thence, whereof the Trojans were sorry of the rappeal. This was the cause wherefore the Trojans lost to have the victory to the which they might never after attain ne come; for fortune was to them contrary. And therefore Virgil saith *Non est misericordia in bello*: that is to say, there is no mercy in battle. A man ought not to take misericord, but take the victory who may get it.

If the Trojans are to blame, though in the main chivalrous, the Greeks are worse. Ulysses and Diomed on an embassy to Troy behave arrogantly and misdeliver their message. Achilles is a downright villain through the treachery he uses to procure the deaths of the two chief Trojan warriors, Hector and Troilus.

Such, then, are the general features of the Lydgate tradition. We must further remember that Shakespeare probably knew Chaucer's *Troilus and Criseyde* at an early age. This poem was regarded as Chaucer's masterpiece in the sixteenth century. Erasmus mentions it approvingly in the *Praise of Folly*, Sidney in his *Defence of Poetry* mentions it alone of Chaucer's works. Now when Cressida appears in the *Troy Book* she is already Troilus's plighted lover; and Lydgate expressly excuses himself from treating their earlier history by saying that Chaucer has already dealt with it. So Shakespeare would perforce take his conception of the pair, in their capacity of lovers, from Chaucer. Now Chaucer treats his theme as a comedy and never gets nearer to authentic tragic feeling than to pathos. But in Lydgate Troilus is anything but a comic figure. He is indeed a model of constancy as in Chaucer; but this constancy goes beyond fidelity in love and includes a ruthless resolution:

> He was alwey feithful just and stable,
> Perseveraunt and of wil inmutable
> Upon what thing he onys set his herte,
> That doubilnes myght hym nat perverte.
>
> (II. 4879–82)

Above all he was a fierce fighter and no Trojan chief came near him as such except Hector.

It would take too long to enumerate further details of Shakespeare's inheritance, but enough has been said to show that it contained a number of paradoxes. The Trojan War was both romantic and fought for an unworthy cause. Some of the fighters were true knights but committed moral errors: some were ignoble. Troilus was both a comic and a grim figure. Cressida was a faithless woman, but the course of her infidelity and the state of mind dictating it could vary very widely. The story of Troilus and Cressida was an integral part of the story of Troy.

Even if we discount the supposed influence of Chapman's *Iliad*, there is still the chance that *Troilus and Cressida* yielded to a contemporary literary fashion as well as looked to the past. That the play's character becomes plain through its belonging to a new type of comedy is the thesis of Oscar J. Campbell's *Comicall Satyre and Shakespeare's 'Troilus and Cressida'*.* When in 1599 a ban was put on satire and epigram, the satirical impulse was diverted to a new type of comedy professing to derive from the personal type, the Attic Old Comedy. Jonson began the mode with *Every Man out of his Humour* in the same year and continued it in *Cynthia's Revels* and *Poetaster*. Marston was the next practitioner in *Antonio and Mellida, Antonio's Revenge, Jack Drum's Entertainment,* and *What You Will*. All these plays leave the reader not serene but 'in an aroused state of scorn at human folly and futility'. Campbell holds that the difficulties of *Troilus and Cressida* vanish if it is read as a satirical comedy of this kind, if we expect it to leave us uneasy and apt to go on criticizing the abuses we see about us. Shakespeare satirized not only Cressida but Troilus, not only Greeks but Trojans. Though not writing a pacifist tract he did attack undisciplined warfare where the generals quarrelled, which was only too common in some late-Elizabethan expeditions.

As a whole the thesis cannot stand and it has been successfully

* San Marino, California, 1938.

challenged. I should myself question several of the premisses on which it rests. Far from lacking serenity after *Every Man out of his Humour*, the reader identifies himself with Jonson's steady belief in good sense and the social norm and rejoices that the various satirized characters have been purged of their ridiculous or wicked peculiarities. Indeed the conversion of Sordido is too ingenuously simple and pious and melodramatic. The play is anything but a problem play. Marston's Antonio plays contain satirical elements, but they are nearer to the revenge play of Kyd than to any conceivable satirical comedy; certainly nearer to *Hamlet* than to *Troilus and Cressida*. They lack indeed the Jonsonian repose, but their unease is quite other than the difficult and complex unease by which *Troilus and Cressida* is characterized. Campbell's thesis fails when applied to this play partly because he misses its complexity. The Trojans may have their faults but they have them differently from the Greeks. Hector may err but he is noble compared with Achilles. And to turn Troilus into an adept in lechery is to wreck one of Shakespeare's masterpieces of characterization and to go flat against what his poetry is telling us. It is not a mere sensualist who, awaiting Cressida, says

> I stalk about her door
> Like a strange soul upon the Stygian banks
> Staying for waftage,

and

> My heart beats thicker than a feverous pulse,
> And all my powers do their bestowing lose
> Like vassalage at unawares encount'ring
> The eye of majesty.

The last words tell of a noble devotion, which we know to be tragically misplaced. But the misplacement does not alter the nobility.

Nevertheless Campbell's thesis is useful in making us think of Jonson and Marston in relation to Shakespeare at this time.

Hamlet somehow gathers body when read with the Antonio plays and the *Malcontent*. The satirical element in *Troilus and Cressida*, though deriving from the medieval treatment of the Troy story, is strengthened by the intellectual massiveness of Jonson and by his vast command of words. Jonson was a stiff pace-setter, and Shakespeare benefited by this stiffness. In particular Shakespeare would hardly have made Thersites what he is without Jonson's stimulus. In many ways Macilente in *Every Man out of his Humour* is unlike Thersites, notably when he begins to take an active part in the plot. But as the satirical commentator he resembles him. Carlo Buffone can do the same job. In this passage, for instance, he speaks very like Thersites:

> I never hungered so much for anything in my life as I do to know our gallants' success at court; now is that lean bald-rib Macilente, that salt villain, plotting some mischievous device and lies a-soaking in their frothy humours like a dry crust, till he has drunk 'em all up. Could the pummice but hold up his eyes at other men's happiness in any reasonable proportion, 'slid the slave were to be loved next heaven, above honour, wealth, rich fare, apparel, wenches, all the delights of the belly and the groin whatever. (v. 4. 23–32)

Finally, Peter Alexander* had adduced a possible contemporary circumstance to explain some of the peculiarities of *Troilus and Cressida*. The cynicism, the scurrility, and the academic tone of some of the speeches could be accounted for, if Shakespeare were writing for the sophisticated audience of the Inns of Court. It is an interesting and attractive theory that may facilitate the first stages of understanding, and it has proved widely acceptable. There is, however, one scene which does not fit. This is III. 2, where Pandarus, Troilus, and Cressida emerge from their own distinctive and dramatic characters and become types: Pandarus as the Bawd, Troilus as Fidelity in Love, Cressida as Falsehood in Love. It is also the one scene that confirms L. C. Knight's† notion

* *Shakespeare's Life and Art*, pp. 195–6.
† *The Times Literary Supplement*, 2 June 1932, p. 408.

that the play is partially akin to the Morality. The scene is quaint and primitive and alien to the sophisticated audience of the Inns of Court. Indeed it resembles in intention those crude informative passages in Elizabethan History Plays where the author seeks to satisfy the appetite for facts likely in a simple audience. It is as if Shakespeare was saying 'I think you have a notion in your heads of Troilus, Cressida, and Pandarus as proverbial persons and you are curious to know how they have become such. Generally, I give you my own version of the story, but in this scene here they are, for your satisfaction, in the guise in which you have habitually pictured them.' First, Troilus says that 'as true as Troilus' will be the chief of all comparisons of constancy, then Cressida says much the same of 'as false as Cressid', and then Pandarus sums up, including himself:

Go to, a bargain made: seal it, seal it; I'll be the witness. Here I hold your hand, here my cousin's. If ever you prove false one to another, since I have taken such pains to bring you together, let all pitiful goers-between be called to the world's end after my name: call them all Pandars. Let all constant men be Troiluses, all false women Cressids, and all brokers-between Pandars. Say, amen!

Here Troilus has quite ceased to be Troy's second Hector, the furious fighter and fiery politician, and is simply the Constant Lover; Cressida has ceased to be the charming and witty, if wanton, Trojan society lady and is simply Female Fickleness; and Pandar is no longer Lord Pandarus, the simpering courtier and kindly sympathizer with Troilus in the extremity of his romantic passion, and has turned into the eternal Common Bawd. To the Elizabethans such transformations would be perfectly natural. An eminent example occurs at the end of the tenth canto of Book Three of the *Fairy Queen*, where Malbecco, once a jealous old man with a recognizable character, is left Timon-like to live in a cave near the sea-shore till he ceases to be a man and becomes Jealousy.

> There dwells he ever, miserable swain,
> Hateful both to himself and every wight,
> Where he through privy grief and horror vain
> Is woxen so deform'd that he has quite
> Forgot he was a man and Jealousy is hight.

But Spenser and his methods, and the Morality tradition, though familiar enough at the Inns of Court of 1602, were not the latest, fashionable things; and Shakespeare's archaic scene comes queerly and yet with wonderful dramatic effect in the midst of matter so much more sophisticated.

I have dwelt so long* on the play's background, because for a play about which opinion is so divided no extrinsic help in interpretation can be spared. I will recapitulate some of the conditions that might have prompted Shakespeare to frame his play in this or that fashion. Most important of all he must have had a certain large conception of the Trojan War, acquired beyond doubt several years before and in all probability fixed deep and firm in his memory by youthful reading. According to it the war was one of the great examples of the ruin wrought by Time, a war fought for an unjust cause but marked by superlative displays of knightly prowess, displays now belonging to an antique age. Next, Shakespeare's conception of a single episode of the war, the loves of Troilus and Cressida, would be rather alien to his general conception of the war and even inconsistent in its parts. The most eminent version was comic, but other versions were satirical. Shakespeare's options here were wide. Thirdly, there was a quite different version of the whole war that contradicted the version he and his contemporaries were used to, that of Homer. It would have been possible, but daring and heterodox, to have adopted it. More important, to do so would have been to deny a firmly seated and perhaps very dear portion of his mental stores. Anyhow, he was aware of the version and took some details from it.

* For another illustration of how Lydgate can explain a difficulty in *Troilus and Cressida* see Appendix C, p. 147.

Fourthly, Shakespeare was exposed to the influence of a biting type of comedy practised just then by his greatest contemporary dramatist. This satirical type was nicely fitted to reinforce the critical temper already strong in the main inherited conception of the Trojan War. Finally, Shakespeare may have had in mind an exceptionally sophisticated audience to which to address his play.

The sum of all these circumstances should be such as to prevent our being at all surprised at any of the ingredients of *Troilus and Cressida*; it should, at this hour of day, have quenched all moanings that Shakespeare was guilty of degrading the high Homeric tradition. It should reassure us that in substance Shakespeare was being decently conventional. But I cannot share the optimism of those critics who have believed that this or that traditional strain or nearer influence gives the entry into the play itself. Indeed, in seeking extrinsic help in understanding *Troilus and Cressida*, I have reached the same conclusion as in studying Shakespeare's History Plays, about which I wrote 'Shakespeare's Histories are more like his own Comedies and Tragedies than like others' Histories'. Some help we may get from Lydgate and Jonson, but more still from Shakespeare's other plays. And in the end the critic is forced to his basic task of interpreting the text: a task whose difficulties and dangers are obvious through a diversity of interpretation as great as of any play of Shakespeare.

Since the character of a play (if it has any consistent character at all) is determined by its opening scenes, I will begin by recording how these scenes in *Troilus and Cressida* strike me.

Everyone would agree that in *Troilus and Cressida* Shakespeare set himself a double theme, that of the Trojan War and that of the loves of the title characters. They would further agree that the two themes are approximated through having as motives a woman, each bad in her own way. It is especially important to remember that Lydgate is strong on the worthlessness of Helen. But more prominent, as the link between the themes, is Troilus himself, who is both lover in the one story and knight in the other.

And again we must remember the surpassing prowess of Troilus in the Lydgate tradition: second only to Hector in the field and having the last word in the council chamber. Shakespeare therefore chose the most effective method of bringing in both themes jointly when he began with Troilus. But he also chose to complicate matters by showing him along with Pandarus, in a comic light inherited from Chaucer. It is unusual comedy, for in it verse and prose are mixed; and this mixture is in itself a pointer to the kind of play it is to be. Troilus speaks verse and Pandarus prose. Troilus is young, very much in love, changeable, taking himself with terrible seriousness. He is ridiculous, and yet he speaks such poetry that we have to take him seriously as well:

> Her bed is India; there she lies, a pearl:
> Between our Ilium and where she resides
> Let it be call'd the wild and wandering flood,
> Ourself the merchant, and this sailing Pandar
> Our doubtful hope, our convoy, and our bark.

This mixture of the ridiculous and the serious is not that proper to comedy. It is comic when the ridiculously romantic excesses of youth are tamed to the terms of good sense. But Pandarus does not stand for good sense and he does not inhabit the same world as Troilus. He is good-natured but he is coarse; and the kind of love that possesses Troilus is quite outside his experience or power of imagination. And so we have the rather bitterly ironical spectacle of two people, both apparently united in their end, yet at bottom conceiving that end in incompatible terms. There is thus much richness in the things presented and much zest in the spectacle. The effect of the alternating verse and prose is inflation and deflation. But what is deflated is in part good, and the deflation is but partly valid. Our responses are thus complicated; and not every spectator likes thus to be played on. Most prefer to know at once just how they stand. Those who enjoy such complication will find the scene a perfect opening: it is masterly done.

When Pandarus goes out, Troilus hears the sounds of war and comments on them in words that both tell us the colour in which the Trojan War will appear and clinch the irony that has already been indicated:

> Peace, you ungracious clamours, peace, rude sounds!
> Fools on both sides! Helen must needs be fair,
> When with your blood you daily paint her thus.
> I cannot fight upon this argument;
> It is too starv'd a subject for my sword.
> But Pandarus – O gods, how do you plague me!
> I cannot come to Cressid but by Pandar;
> And he's as tetchy to be woo'd to woo
> As she is stubborn-chaste against all suit.

Troilus speaks about Helen in a way that grossly contradicts his words about her in the Trojan council scene (II. 2); and we can take our choice between saying that he is in a highly changeable mood and saying that he here speaks out of character because Shakespeare needs just here to tell us how he will picture the war, and Troilus is handy. Anyhow the two main themes are brought in by the simultaneous mention of the two motivating ladies: while Troilus's disillusion over Helen and his illusion over Cressida as 'stubborn-chaste' are successfully ironical. Finally Aeneas enters, and Troilus shows his mutability by consenting to enter the battle in spite of having just said he 'cannot fight upon this argument'.

The second scene of the play, between Cressida and Pandarus, shows the two 'arguments', of love and of war, and the passing of the main Trojan warriors, supporters of the second 'argument'. Pandarus and Cressida talk in prose together; they are of the same world. Pandarus, in his silly story about the hairs in Troilus's chin, lets us see the triviality of Helen and her courtiers; Cressida by her mechanically witty interruptions shows herself an efficient society woman without depth of feeling. It is directly after Pandarus's story, and with ironical intent, that the Greek warriors are made to pass by. The importance of Hector among them has been made clear during the whole scene. The tone of the scene is comic, with a strong mixture of satire. Deflation is the rule; and it prepares by contrast for the highly inflated scene that follows, the war council of the Greeks.

So far the intention of the play has been pretty plain; but what are we now to make of the ample rhetoric that flows from the mouths of Agamemnon, Nestor, and Ulysses for over two hundred lines from the beginning? Van Doren hates it so much that he calls the style of the whole play 'loud, brassy, and abandoned'. Ulysses's speech on *degree* is 'merely as rant, tremendous'. Others see in this same speech one of the high places in Shakespeare's most considered and serious writing, while the scene itself becomes a weighty and earnest piece of political theorizing. I cannot accept either opinion. The style throughout is quite deliberate and not in the least 'abandoned'; and yet Shakespeare was not writing in the full passion of earnestness, was not quite sunk in what he did, but (to alter the metaphor) had his tongue at least part way in his cheek. He does in fact continue his method of inflation and deflation; only here, in addition to the anticipatory deflation of the previous scene, the inflated style contains, through its excess, its own deflatory self-criticism. Shakespeare does in fact slightly parody himself, but he enjoys such writing and knows that it is grand stuff though somewhat burlesque: with the same implication (but without the depreciation and apology) as Eliot's comment in *East Coker* on his lapse into an earlier way of writing:

> That was a way of putting it – not very satisfactory:
> A periphrastic study in a worn-out poetical fashion.

Now the interesting thing (and Van Doren has noted it) is that the style from which the speeches in question take off is that of certain parts of *Henry V*. The speeches are rhetorical rather than conversational, containing long sentences, frequent synonyms or near-synonyms, and an unusually latinized vocabulary. Here are a few places in *Henry V* that come near to the rhetorical style of *Troilus and Cressida*:

> O pardon! since a crooked figure may
> Attest in little place a million;
> And let us, ciphers to this great accompt,
> On your imaginary forces work.
> Suppose within the girdle of these walls
> Are now confin'd two mighty monarchies,
> Whose high upreared and abutting fronts
> The perilous narrow ocean parts asunder.

> And, to relief of lazars and weak age,
> Of indigent faint souls past corporal toil . . .

> And never noted in him any study,
> Any retirement, any sequestration
> From open haunts and popularity.

> The severals and unhidden passages
> Of his true titles to some certain dukedoms . . .

> For government, though high and low and lower,
> Put into parts doth keep in one consent,
> Congreeing in a full and natural close
> Like music. Therefore doth heaven divide
> The state of man in divers functions
> Setting endeavour in continual motion;
> To which is fixed as an aim or butt
> Obedience.

Ulysses's speech on degree echoes in many ways the Archbishop's speech on the commonwealth of the bees, actually hinting at it in

> When that the general is not like the hive
> To whom the foragers shall all repair,
> What honey is expected?

But of all the speeches in *Henry V* the nearest in style to *Troilus and Cressida* is Burgundy's in v. 2 on the plight of the land of France, which may suggest that the occurrence of the word *deracinate* here and in Ulysses's speech on degree, and nowhere else in Shakespeare, is more than an accident.

The resemblances between these speeches and parts of *Henry V* count the more, because there is nothing like them in *Julius Caesar*, the political play that comes between. Antony there may not be an amiable character, and Brutus may be a poor politician, but there is not the slightest suggestion that politicians are windbags. But in *Henry V* the spirit of criticism plays on the minor characters who are politicians and may even extend to the man of action in general, if only unconsciously. In *Troilus and Cressida* this spirit comes right into the open and is intensified.

But though the common tone of the Greeks' speeches is inflated, there is scope for dramatic differentiation within it. Agamemnon is slow-witted and genuinely pompous: witness his lack of initiative as a commander throughout the play and some of his later speeches. Not for nothing does Patroclus, for Achilles's amusement, assume Agamemnon's 'topless deputation . . . with terms unsquared, which from the tongue of roaring Typhon dropp'd would seem hyperboles'. After Hector's challenge has been delivered, later in this scene, Agamemnon can think of nothing subtler than to tell Achilles of it; and it remains for Ulysses to turn it to good account. For Agamemnon's continued inflation take his few words at the beginning of IV. 5, when Ajax stands ready for the duel:

> Here art thou in appointment fresh and fair,
> Anticipating time with starting courage.
> Give with thy trumpet a loud note to Troy,
> Thou dreadful Ajax, that the appalled air
> May pierce the head of the great combatant
> And hale him hither.

The inflation of Nestor's style is perhaps more on the side of proverbial amplification and suggests the old man as well as the pompous politician. Ulysses's is more complicated. He can be direct enough if he cares, as when he describes Patroclus acting Nestor and the mirth of Achilles, who cries

> O, enough, Patroclus,
> Or give me ribs of steel! I shall split all
> In pleasure of my spleen.

His is an assumed inflation, an example of a good politician's adaptability to his surroundings. And he knows exactly what he is doing. His speech on degree is a cunning piece of rhetorical generalization in the current style initiated by Agamemnon and Nestor, splendid and beating them on their own ground, and leading on to something concrete, a reference to Achilles, the chief offender against discipline. Through this speech, so correct in sentiment yet so exciting to a later age as an epitome of contemporary commonplaces, so lacking in personal passion and yet so enchanting in its golden and leisured orotundity, Ulysses sets up (as he was to maintain and increase) his pre-eminence among the Greek leaders. When he speaks of the contempt of Achilles and others for staff work,

> So that the ram that batters down the wall,
> For the great swing and rudeness of his poise,
> They place before his hand that made the engine,
> Or those that with the fineness of their souls
> By reason guide his execution,

he knows that he is the one leader with an effective fineness of soul and that his mission is to get the most effective ram, Achilles, into action again.

As Ulysses finishes this criticism of the Greek officers on strike, the trumpet sounds for Aeneas's delivery of Hector's challenge. At first appearance Aeneas's words, so taut and sprightly, offer an utter contrast to the Greeks' sluggish and protracted oratory. The Trojans, he says, are

> Courtiers as free, as debonair, unarm'd,
> As bending angels; that's their fame in peace:
> But when they would seem soldiers, they have galls,
> Good arms, strong joints, true swords; and, Jove's accord,
> Nothing so full of heart.

That might be well enough by itself, but what of the challenge, itself?

> Hector, in view of Trojans and of Greeks,
> Shall make it good, or do his best to do it:
> He hath a lady, wiser, fairer, truer,
> Than ever Greek did compass in his arms;
> And will to-morrow with his trumpet call
> Midway between your tents and walls of Troy,
> To rouse a Grecian that is true in love.
> If any come, Hector shall honour him;
> If none, he'll say in Troy when he retires
> The Grecian dames are sunburnt and not worth
> The splinter of a lance.

Certainly the style here is fresher, quicker, more energetic than the Greek rhetoric, and intentionally so. But can we take it that Shakespeare is, as it were, quite on the Trojan side and that he sets up Trojan forthrightness against Greek pomposity and cunning? I fear not. Aeneas's energy, like the Greeks' magniloquence, carries within it its own agent of deflation. Although much of the Middle Ages survived into the Elizabethan age, although a traditional romantic episode like the wager can pass accepted and uncriticized in a romantic play like *Cymbeline*, this presentation of *amour courtois*, in a context such as Shakespeare has created, can only be slightly absurd, a piece of engaging if you will, but not serious, antiquarianism. Puntarvolo and his surroundings in *Every Man out of his Humour* are a greatly exaggerated version of the same notion; and the Baron of Bradwardine in *Waverley* is very close to Shakespeare's Trojans. The Trojans have admirable qualities but they are antiquated in their ideas and they lack the realism of the Greeks who, though in their way inefficient, are at least modern and free from the antiquarian illusions of chivalry. The ineffectiveness of the Trojans' admirable qualities can, as the play proceeds, hover on the borders of the tragic and the ridiculous. If we need confirmation that Hector's challenge is not to be taken in full seriousness we can find it in the speeches of Agamemnon and Nestor. Agamemnon's

> And may that soldier a mere recreant prove
> That means not, hath not, or is not in love!
> If then one is, or hath, or means to be,
> That one meets Hector –

or Nestor's

>   tell him that my lady
> Was fairer than his grandam and as chaste –

are surely not to be taken in all seriousness.

The scene ends with Nestor and Ulysses remaining behind. Ulysses finds Nestor useful as a political ally and tells him his scheme to put Hector's challenge up to a lottery, which shall be rigged so as to fall to Ajax. Achilles, through jealousy, may thus be stirred to action. Ulysses thus emerges as the indubitable motive force of the Greek camp.

The next scene (II. I), which the editors should never have separated from the last by an act division, introduces us to the factious Greek leader and to Thersites. It is pure comedy, embittered by Thersites's exuberantly foul vocabulary. To make Thersites into a chorus, the authentic commentator on the play's action, is ridiculous. His function is that of a Fool, to give a twist to every action and every motive. And this twist is always to the vile and the loathsome. Sometimes he hits the mark, at others he is wide of it. His exclamation at the end of v. 2, 'Lechery, lechery; still wars and lechery; nothing else holds fashion', has been taken as a choric comment on the play as a whole. Actually, in its context, it refers to Diomed and Patroclus alone; but Troilus, Aeneas, and Ulysses have just gone out, and to the last two it applies not at all and to the first only in small part. Thersites is a consistently bitter element in the play, not a coloured glass through which we watch it. His genuine if diseased curiosity makes his ubiquity credible; and his ubiquity helps to join one part of the Greek camp with another. For instance in the present scene he shows his knowledge that Ulysses with Nestor is the true motive force among the Greeks and he tells Achilles and Ajax so:

> There's Ulysses and old Nestor . . . yoke you like draught-oxen and make you plough up the wars. . . . 'To, Achilles! To, Ajax!'

Achilles, the lolling bully for the moment, but with a keen practical eye to his self-interest, is brilliantly drawn. He defends Thersites against Ajax with hulking leisureliness, but speeds up at the end when he speaks of the challenge and his own possible part in it, his eyes narrowing in self-centred jealousy.

> *Achilles*: Marry, this, sir, is proclaim'd through all our host:
>   That Hector, by the fifth hour of the sun,
>   Will with a trumpet 'twixt our tents and Troy
>   To-morrow morning call some knight to arms
>   That hath a stomach; and such a one that dare
>   Maintain – I know not what: 'tis trash. Farewell.
> *Ajax*: Farewell. Who shall answer him?
> *Achilles*: I know not: 'tis put to lottery; otherwise
>   He knew his man.
> *Ajax*: Oh, meaning you. I will go learn more of it.

The next scene shows Priam and his sons in council. It is of almost the same length as the Greek council scene and is an obvious companion piece. But it is more difficult to interpret; and before attempting its difficulties I will note some of the undoubted or probable results of the comparison Shakespeare wants us to make.

First (and this is no more than a probability) Aeneas and Antenor are absent from the Trojan council, which consists only of Priam and his sons; it is thus antique and patriarchal in contrast to the more normal mixed council of the Greeks. Secondly, the Trojans, though beginning with a matter of concrete policy, whether to keep or to return Helen, go back to the great abstract moral questions, while the Greeks had never left practical politics. Even Ulysses's general doctrine of degree was never detached from its practical application. As well as being more moral the Trojans allow a larger scope to the emotions. Thirdly, as Ulysses emerged as the virtual leader of the Greeks, so Troilus emerges as the dynamic power of the Trojans. Hector rebukes Troilus and Paris for being young men in a hurry; yet it is Troilus's counsel that prevails, and (most important) he speaks incomparably the finest poetry. Hector, for all his talents and his magnanimity, does in effect match Achilles as the battering-ram rather than the hand directing it, only, as it were, one gifted with brains which it does not use. Troilus, like Ulysses, is the guiding hand. And Troilus and Ulysses remain the dominant characters throughout. To establish this important position I will anticipate and give two illustrations from later parts of the play. First, it is Ulysses, the wisest of the Greeks, that describes Troilus to Agamemnon. Now we know already that in the Trojan tradition used by Shakespeare Hector and Troilus were the two first Trojan commanders, with the others far behind them. Ulysses makes Troilus the more formidable and single-minded,

> a true knight,
> Not yet mature, yet matchless, firm of words,
> Speaking in deeds and deedless in his tongue,
> Not soon provok'd nor being provok'd soon calm'd:
> His heart and hand both open and both free,
> For what he has he gives, what thinks he shows;
> Yet gives he not till judgement guide his bounty
> Nor dignifies an impair thought with breath:
> Manly as Hector but more dangerous;
> For Hector in his blaze of wrath subscribes

> To tender objects, but he in heat of action
> Is more vindicative than jealous love.

Secondly, in one of the play's culminating places, if not the culminating place itself, the revelation of Cressida's infidelity, it is Ulysses who is Troilus's companion. Shakespeare wanted us to think of them together; and the things the two stand for must surely be an important part of the play's meaning.

But at this point the question cannot but intrude: what has become of the romantic lover of the play's first scene, the young man slightly comic though with the hint of profounder feelings? To claim a psychological consistency would be possible: young men very much in love are in fact able to conduct practical business efficiently. But to use such a possibility as an aesthetic justification would be to flout Aristotle's just preference for probable impossibilities over possible improbabilities. The change from the harassed and mercurial lover to the fiercely resolute and overmastering young commander is too violent to be swallowed without effort. It is very greatly mitigated in the acting, because sufficient has happened between Troilus's two appearances to induce a good measure of oblivion. But it cannot be taken with ultimate ease; and I fancy that one reason why the play fails to satisfy us completely is that Troilus as a character is made to bear too much, that his double part of romantic and unfortunate lover and of leading spirit among the Trojan commanders taxes the spectator's aesthetic credulity beyond its powers. Shakespeare here may have been tempted to try the impossible through loyalty to his originals, Chaucer and Lydgate, who give such different versions of Troilus.

I come now to the difficulties of the scene itself: the interpretation of the Trojan debate. And first I had better summarize it. Priam announces the Greek offer to make peace, wiping out all old scores, if Helen is returned to them, and asks Hector's opinion. Hector says that though personally fearless of the Greeks, he is prone on grounds of general policy to consider the actual event.

Helen in herself is not worth the results of her seizure. Therefore let her go back. Troilus breaks in violently to the effect that it is an insult to Priam's honour to reduce motives to a scale of reason. Helenus contradicts him; and Troilus scornfully proves how reason in Helenus teaches him to run away. Hector repeats that Helen is not worth the cost of holding her. Troilus retorts that worth is not in the object but in the minds of those considering the object. Hector passionately asserts the principle of self-value and that it is mad idolatry to make the service greater than the god. Troilus evades the argument and puts forward another: that it is dishonourable to go back on our commitments. The Trojans consented to Paris's expedition and they must back him up. Then he shifts his argument again: Helen is not worthless but a peerless beauty; she is self-valuable and those responsible for her other kind of value must not cheapen it by lowering their first esteem. Cassandra breaks in, foretells Troy's ruin if Helen stays, and goes out. Hector asks Troilus if fear of failure in a bad cause does not move him. Troilus replies that we must not think of the event. Moreover Cassandra is mad, and her madness must not compromise a course hallowed by the engagement of the honour of all. Paris then echoes Troilus's pleas, interrupted by Priam, who tells him he is an interested party. Hector compliments Paris and Troilus on their speeches but says they are nevertheless superficial, not grounded on ethical truth but the one on lust and the other on revenge. Ethically, there is a great overriding argument: the sanctity of marriage based on natural law and international consent. The plea that it is dishonourable to go back on a commitment is false, if that commitment was in itself wicked. To persist in it is but to augment the crime. The plain morality is that Helen should be returned; and yet, Hector says, with a surprising turn, he agrees with Paris and Troilus in their resolution to keep her, for it is a matter affecting the honour of each of them. Troilus is delighted and, dropping any pretence at argument, enthusiastically proclaims the glory for which Helen is the pretext.

The scene advances the action not at all; its dramatic purpose is to depict the minds of the two principal Trojans, Hector and Troilus. And it does so through a contrast that would have been plain to any educated Elizabethan. The above summary should have shown that Troilus is not strong in argument: his understanding is ruled by his emotions. He finds plenty of reasons why Helen should be kept, but they are reasons hastily shuffled together to support a resolution already taken. He refuses to use his understanding on the fundamental ethics of the case. Thus, in Elizabethan terms, he is defective in wit but strong in will. Hector is just the opposite. He has a perfectly clear understanding and recognizes unerringly the fundamental ethics of the case and the prejudiced understanding of his brothers. But there is a divorce between his wit, in which he is so strong, and his will, in which he is so defective. He is a plain case of 'video meliora proboque, deteriora sequor'. And as it is the will that directs action, Hector as a directing force of the Trojans must yield to Troilus.

Such an opinion of Hector will provoke opposition because there is so set a prejudice for the opinion of him as the soul of honour, the one really good man in the play, tragically murdered by Achilles. But I simply cannot see how we can gloze over the terrible rift in him between his understanding and his will, which Shakespeare shows us with an emphasis so strong as sometimes to stun rather than awaken the critics' perceptions. Nor is this picture of Hector's fatally divided mind, unmistakably evident, as I believe, from the present scene, unsupported. In IV. 5, when Ulysses and Hector talk, Hector, in reply to Ulysses's assertion that Troy's towers will fall, says

> I must not believe you.
> There they stand yet, and modestly I think
> The fall of every Phrygian stone will cost
> A drop of Grecian blood. The end crowns all,
> And that old common arbitrator, Time,
> Will one day end it.

Hector does in fact believe it, and yet he says he must not. Then there is v. 3, where Hector leaves Troy for the last time. Cassandra in trying to keep him back uses exactly the same arguments Hector uses in the council scene for sending Helen back; and we are meant to think of both scenes together. Here Cassandra argues that his vow to fight has proved wrong and unreasonable in view of the adverse omens and that he ought to go back on it. Just as with his understanding he knew that for the general good Helen should be restored, so he must now know that it is for the general good that he should avoid fighting on this fatal day. Again his will follows not his understanding but the emotional direction of his sense of honour. In the same scene Hector shows his practical ineffectiveness when he treats Troilus as a boy when clearly he has ceased to be one. Troilus in his turn rebukes his vice of excessive generosity in the field, a vice that favours the enemy overmuch. Hector, for all his nobility, stands for a double ineffectiveness: personally for a mind divided between reasonable, realistically moral, action and unreasoning point of honour; symbolically, for the anachronistic continuance of the chivalric code into a world which has abandoned it.

My opinion of Hector gets some confirmation also from Shakespeare's originals, Lydgate and Caxton. There is a scene in Lydgate (II. 2063–3318) which is so close to the Trojan council in Shakespeare that he must have had some memory of it. The occasion is different from Shakespeare and is of the discussion Priam holds with his sons after he has got the sanction of his regular council to seek to avenge the abduction of Hesione; and it follows Lydgate's earnest reprimand of Priam for not being content with his present prosperity.* Priam begins with a passionate plea for vengeance and calls on Hector to back him up. Hector speaks in much the same way as in Shakespeare but with arguments in reverse order and with the opposite conclusion. He

* The corresponding scene in Caxton is much shorter, less impressive, and less moralized.

begins by professing warmly his belief in the obligation to promote chivalry and his desire for revenge. Nevertheless, he goes on, you must consider the event or end. The Greeks are actually stronger; and though we may begin well the end may be ill. Further, Hesione is not worth the risk of all their lives:

> And though also myn aunte Exioun
> Ageyn al right be holde of Thelamoun,
> It is not good for her redempcioun
> To putte us alle to destruccioun.
> I rede not to beyen hir half so dere.

Paris disagrees, and, having recounted his dream of the three goddesses, proposes stealing a Greek woman and exchanging her for Hesione. Deiphobus supports Paris. Helenus opposes Paris because he knows by his divination that Troy will be destroyed if Paris goes. At this speech all sit silent and troubled, till at last Troilus 'young, fresh, and lusty' springs up and chides his family for being so cast down. He furiously attacks Helenus for a coward and scorns the truth of divination. Let Helenus allow 'lusty knights' to prove their valour in battle and to be avenged on their enemies. The whole gathering praise Troilus's high spirit, and not even Hector opens his mouth against him. Later, when Cassandra hears of Paris's success and Helen's arrival, she condemns the adultery in words that were quoted early in this chapter. In this scene of Priam discussing his proposed vengeance on the Greeks with his sons, Hector shows the best understanding and foresight but his will is quite borne down by Troilus. The position therefore that Shakespeare's Hector was strong in wit but not in will is confirmed by the corresponding scene in Lydgate.

Hector's other vices, the covetousness that causes his death and his disastrous excess of magnanimity in the field, have been mentioned already. The first is not stressed by Shakespeare, who merely makes Hector say, when he sees one 'enter in sumptuous armour', that he has a liking for that armour. But when Troilus accuses him of a dangerous and excessive magnanimity we tend to justify the accusation, and with Lydgate in the background can be confirmed in so doing.

To return to the Trojan council scene as a whole, it differs from the corresponding Greek scene in being written in swifter and tauter verse and in touching on matters which Shakespeare, having them more at heart, treats with a nearer and more intimate fervour. The irony of Troilus arguing that value rests in the valuer and not in the thing valued is terrible when we apply his argument to his own fate at the hands of Cressida, and looks forward to the play's emotional climax. And the same question, in the department of war, was obviously haunting Shakespeare through its occurrence so prominently in *Hamlet*; for it is precisely this question that Hamlet discusses when on his way to embark for England he meets the forces of Fortinbras (IV. 4): first with Fortinbras's captain, and then with himself in his soliloquy beginning 'How all occasions . . .'. Each scene may grow clearer in the light of the other's treatment of this common subject; so I will make a comparison. The episode in *Hamlet* is of the hero's seeing Fortinbras and his soldiers pass by on their way to fight the Poles for the possession of a piece of land not worth five ducats' rent or even purchase. While talking to Fortinbras's captain, Hamlet is critical of the coming contest:

> This is the imposthume of much wealth and peace,
> That inward breaks and shows no cause without
> Why the man dies.

In other words the bloodshed has no higher function than to get rid of an excess of blood in the body politic, of population in the state. But this thought is not single; it is fiercely denied in the soliloquy that follows. For Hamlet proceeds to take sides against the ethics both of Lydgate's and of Shakespeare's Hector by condemning a precise thinking on the event. Fortinbras was right in cocking a snook at the invisible event and considering present glory. And he, Hamlet, is the more despicable in his shirking the glory of present action, for having a much more compelling cause. True greatness consists not in doing something for a trivial issue but in exalting that issue through turning it into a matter of honour. Helen in the Trojan council has exactly the same position as the barren piece of land in Hamlet's questionings: her final justification is that she is an argument of honour. The most interesting thing that emerges from the comparison is the contrasted positions of Hector and Hamlet. Hector is clear on the ethical side and in theory opposes the ethics of Hamlet's soliloquy; but in practice he follows Hamlet's advice. Hamlet is tortured on the ethical side and ends by opposing the theories of Hector. But in practice he follows Hector's theories with a pertinacity that argues some unconscious acceptance. Hamlet's conflict is deeper, nobler, more interesting than Hector's. With his conscious mind he flogs himself into the belief that action about a triviality is justified; with his deeper self he can consent to embrace only the worthiest of causes. The conflict is fierce, and Hamlet is a tragic figure. Hector reasons clearly and then weakly allows custom and convention to bear down his reasoning – which he has put up with a kind of frivolous academicism knowing that he will not follow it out. In the division of his mind he is no more than a pathetic figure: a great man of action without ultimate conviction about the grounds for that action; lacking at once the ruthless practical impulse of Troilus and the deep emotions of Hamlet.

But if Shakespeare is nearer emotionally to the problems that exercise the Trojan council, he treats the Trojans no less critically than he treated the Greeks. The Trojans have more capacious minds, deeper feelings, and a freer speech than the Greeks, yet they achieve less. Out of Greek pomposity and cunning a line of action has emerged; all the Trojans can do is to accept the news of a picturesque but pointless challenge and to decide to go on as before.

By the end of the scene just discussed, the temper of the play has been made clear; and from now on I can abbreviate. II. 3 takes us back to the Greeks, to the abuse of Thersites and to the leaders feeding the pride of Ajax to provoke Achilles. The tone is mainly comic; but Thersites's 'all the argument is a whore and a cuckold' is a satirical comment on Troilus's description of Helen in the last scene as

> a Grecian queen, whose youth and freshness
> Wrinkles Apollo's and makes stale the morning.

In the next scene (III. 1), when Pandarus visits Helen to ask her help in excusing Troilus's expected absence from the royal supper table that evening, the Trojans get their turn of satire and ridicule. Paris's servant is insolent to Lord Pandarus – an upsetting of degree; Pandarus's conversation with Helen and Paris degrades the 'argument' of the war and those about her through satirizing contemporary affectations of speech in the most frivolous section of high society. The scene leads on to a greater: the coming together of Troilus and Cressida through the offices of Pandarus, ending with the curious episode, already mentioned, of the three characters ceasing to be themselves and becoming types. Now that Troilus has won Cressida, his love has shed its comic side and has become wholly tragic – as befits the powerful character revealed in the council scene. The only plane on which the two can meet is the sensual; and for a first meeting this can suffice them. But the lovely poetry Troilus speaks and the speculations his passion prompts mark him off decisively from the world of Cressida and Pandarus. Tragic irony reaches its height when hearing of Cressida's nervous and sensual flutter from Pandarus he says:

> Even such a passion doth embrace my bosom.
> My heart beats thicker than a feverous pulse,
> And all my powers do their bestowing lose
> Like vassalage at unawares encount'ring
> The eye of majesty.

He is doubly deceived: his own passion is not at all such as Cressida's, and she is anything but the regal character he makes her out. Anyhow, the fortunes and the mind of Troilus have greatly advanced in prominence.

It is partly to match this prominence that the next scene exists. It begins with a brief account of Calchas obtaining his request to have Cressida exchanged for Antenor,* but its larger substance is Ulysses's plea with Achilles to be active once more. And through it Ulysses's pre-eminence among the Greeks is increased and confirmed. He is in charge. He makes the other Greek leaders pass by Achilles's tent and greet him coldly, and himself remains behind to have his say. Here he is at the height of his powers. His policy is consummate. He introduces the desired topic, first by his device of reading something in a book. Then, instead of applying the moral to Achilles direct he cites Ajax as the spectacle of what chance can do to advance a mediocrity into momentary glory. Achilles, envious of Ajax, is likely to be thrown off his guard and to be the less prepared for Ulysses's application of the moral to himself. Ulysses's lie about the lottery, 'an act that very chance doth throw upon him', when actually he had rigged it himself, is slipped in with the perfection of cool casualness. In his culminating speech on Time he clothes his worldly wisdom with a surpassing eloquence: an eloquence which, not to be degraded, demands as auditor an Achilles of superior mental capacity to the Achilles of the rest of the play; an Achilles whom Ulysses, even though partly in flattery, calls 'thou great and complete man' and who, before seeing Ulysses, had spoken nobly and intelligently on the problem of reputation. In this the highest reach of Ulysses's eloquence we are surely meant to contrast his doctrine of honour with the corresponding doctrine of Troilus, his peer among the Trojans. For all his eloquence Ulysses's doctrine of

---

* It is a good piece of craft that Diomed should have a double charge: to fetch Cressida and to make sure that Hector stands by his challenge. The two main themes are thus brought together.

honour is purely selfish and materialistic. The virtue that is bidden not to seek remuneration of the thing it was has nothing ethical about it and is no more than the crude glory that feeds human pride. It is related to no abstract ideal. Troilus, though muddled in his notion of honour, is an idealist. Honour is related to a standard external to the individual. There cannot be too much of it, and even if it is in the eye of the beholder and not in the object, the eye is that of all beholders not just that of the one isolated self-centred person. Each type of honour shows up poorly when measured by the merits of the other.

The natures of the two sides in the war have now been fully developed in isolation; Cressida is due to be transferred from one side to another: so henceforth the two sides and the two themes will be mainly treated together. There is much business to be got through, and the play proceeds more hastily. In the next scene, IV. 1, Diomed on his mission to Troy to bring back Cressida talks with Aeneas and Paris. The quality and intention of these conversations are not very plain. Aeneas and Diomed mix fraternization with defiance in a conventionally heroic way. Does Shakespeare intend any satire here? I think not; and when Paris says in comment

> This is the most despiteful gentle greeting,
> The noblest hateful love that e'er I heard of,

any satire is at the expense of Paris's affected language. If this conversation is not satirical, its point will be to prepare the spectator by its martial tone for the battle scenes at the end of the play. The bitter words of Diomed to Paris about Helen are not too easy to justify either. Helen has come in for plenty of criticism, and Diomed only reinforces a way of feeling we know already.

The next three scenes, IV. 2, 3, and 4, are all transacted in Pandarus's house and should be treated as one. They tell of the lovers after their night together, the fetching of Cressida, and of the lovers' farewell. They are part comic, part pathetic: not tragic, because Troilus thinks he can trust Cressida and that he can visit her among the Greeks. They are scenes splendidly suited to the stage, very varied in passions, full of living characterization. For instance when Cressida in her grief at parting calls herself 'a woful Cressid 'mongst the merry Greeks', we feel that even then the thought flashes through her that the merry Greeks may compensate for what she is losing. Troilus behaves with dignity, already an older man than the youth of the play's opening scene: a clear analogy with Hamlet.

The next is a long scene, bringing first Cressida with Diomed and then Hector with his supporters to the Greek camp. It is nodal, uniting the play's several veins; and that it should be in the main comic or inflated is highly significant. Agamemnon's pompous opening has been quoted already. It is capped by Ajax:

> Thou, trumpet, there's my purse.
> Now crack thy lungs and split thy brazen pipe.
> Blow, villain, till thy sphered bias cheek
> Outswell the colic of puff'd Aquilon.
> Come, stretch thy chest and let thy eyes spout blood:
> Thou blow'st for Hector.

It might almost be Ancient Pistol speaking. The episode of Cressida kissed by all the Greek leaders (except Ulysses) is broadly comic. The single fight between Hector and Ajax and most of the conversations between Greeks and Trojans after its tame conclusion are not exactly comic but stylized and a little quaint. Shakespeare is, as it were, writing between inverted commas, consciously giving his shorthand version of the antique matter of Troy. Hector maintains his character. He is nonchalant about the terms of the fight and warms up only when Achilles would bully him. Let those who question this deliberate antique quaintness compare Hector's speech to Ajax after the fight (119–38) with any of Hector's previous speeches, and they surely will find an altered style. Or can they take this of Hector's as the full Shake-sperean seriousness?

> Not Neoptolemus so mirable,
> On whose bright crest Fame with her loud'st Oyes
> Cries 'This is he' could promise to himself
> A thought of added honour torn from Hector.

But two characters are exempt from the inflation, the comedy, and the antique quaintness alike. The first is Troilus, whose dejected look causes Agamemnon to ask who he is and Ulysses to testify so splendidly to his surpassing merit and courage. Till he is left alone with Ulysses at the end of the scene, he speaks once only: to tell Hector to fight more fiercely. His silence separates him from the rest. The second is Ulysses, who towers right above the other Greeks in good sense and acute or sympathetic perception and he speaks in the full Shakespearean idiom. He sees through Cressida instantly, while the other Greek leaders make fools of themselves. His brief talk with Hector touches the issue of the whole war in contrast with the petty chivalric courtesies or pretences that make up the other conversation. His brief talk with Troilus at the end requires a longer note. Herè are the lines.

> *Troilus*: My Lord Ulysses, tell me, I beseech you,
>   In what place of the field doth Calchas keep?
> *Ulysses*: At Menelaus' tent, most princely Troilus.
>   There Diomed doth feast with him to-night;
>   Who neither looks upon the heaven nor earth
>   But gives all gaze and bent of amorous view
>   On the fair Cressid.
> *Troilus*: Shall I, sweet lord, be bound to you so much,
>   After we part from Agamemnon's tent,
>   To bring me thither?
> *Ulysses*:   You shall command me, sir.
>   As gentle tell me, of what honour was
>   This Cressida in Troy? Had she no lover there
>   That wails her absence?

> *Troilus*: O, sir, to such as boasting show their scars
> A mock is due. Will you walk on, my lord?
> She was belov'd, she lov'd; she is and doth:
> But still sweet love is food for fortune's tooth.

First, it is significant that the two characters who stood aloof from the rest should remain behind. Not only does their exchange of words at so prominent a place confirm their eminence over all the other characters, but its exquisite courtliness and simplicity show that these two arch-enemies, chief sources of strength on either side, are drawn to each other. Troilus instinctively chooses Ulysses as his confidant over Cressida; Ulysses has understood everything (and much more than Troilus yet knows) and in sympathy tries to show he knows and in so doing to enlighten. No passage in Shakespeare renders better a subtle and beautiful human relationship. It should among other things guard against the all too prevalent error that in this play Shakespeare abandoned his normal standards of sweetness and light for the bitter cynicism of Thersites. But I do not wish to sentimentalize either Troilus or Ulysses. Both are set with unbending resolution on their objects: Troilus on love and honour; Ulysses on practical politics. It is partly through admiration of the other's singleness of purpose that there is mutual attraction.

The next scene, v. 1, which in spite of the act-division follows without a pause, is deflatory. Thersites is at the top of his form. Achilles's bragging promise to meet Hector tomorrow in the field comes to nothing, because he has had a letter from Polyxena.

The next scene, v. 2, crowns the play. It happens at night and it shows Troilus and Ulysses watching the love-passage between Cressida and Diomed; both pairs being watched by Thersites. It includes not only Troilus's terrible suffering and schizophrenia but his self-cure through turning that portion of his mind which, against the evidence of his senses, continues to love and idolize Cressida into hatred for Diomed, a hatred which can find vent in

78

action. This mutation, often overlooked, is essential for understanding the play's true course.

In richness of content this scene far surpasses all others in the play. In *Shakespeare's Last Plays* I wrote on the different planes of reality in those plays, maintaining that a sense of several possible planes was here a major theme, though in a subordinate way Shakespeare had shown this sense from the first. And I instanced among others the present scene in *Troilus and Cressida*. Diomed and Cressida inhabit with obtuse and unreflecting singleness of purpose the world of the senses. In that world each is equally on the make for himself. Ulysses inhabits the world of convention and practises the maximum of sympathy possible within that world. Samuel Butler would have classed him with the Higher Ydgrunites. Troilus inhabits a world largely emotional; and conflicting emotions threaten to destroy for him the mind's normal traffic. He does in fact for a brief time inhabit two incompatible worlds. But the self-control he maintained while the evidence for one of these incompatible worlds was accumulating enables him to subject the incompatibility to his will and to transform one incompatible into something that can fit into the rest of his experience. Thersites inhabits a world uniformly sordid, in which all motives are monotonously degraded; it contains no particle of pity, and he is as brutal in his comment on Troilus's conflict ('Will he swagger himself out on's own eyes?') as in any of his ranker scurrilities concerning the Greeks.

This multiplication of planes of reality beyond anything similar elsewhere in the play threatens to destroy the play's internal harmony because it includes a type of feeling not included elsewhere. I must speak about that feeling and explain why (like Shylock in the *Merchant of Venice*) it does not in fact fulfil its threat.

Charles Williams in his interesting but speculative treatment of *Troilus and Cressida* in his *English Poetic Mind*★ speaks well of the

★Oxford, 1932, pp. 59–61.

type of experience Troilus undergoes in this scene, contrasting it
with other types found in the play elsewhere:

The crisis which Troilus endured is one common to all men; it is in a
sense the only interior crisis worth talking about. It is that in which every
nerve of the body, every consciousness of the mind, shrieks that something cannot be. Only it is. . . .

There is a world where our mothers are unsoiled and Cressida is his;
there is a world where our mothers are soiled and Cressida is given to
Diomed. . . .

Agamemnon and Nestor had made orations about the disappoint-
ments of life, the failure of 'the ample proposition that hope makes', and
the need of courage and patience. Ulysses had answered by pointing out
that degree and order were being lost, and had described what happens
when degree is lost. It was all very wise, very noble, talk. But in Troilus
the thing has happened: the plagues, portents, and mutinies have begun
to 'divert and crack, rend and deracinate' his being.

Charles Williams is right in seeing this different order of emotion,
vouched for, of course, by a more intense way of writing. In
commenting on the Trojan council scene I said that Shakespeare
was now writing on a subject of debate which he had more at
heart and which he treated with a nearer and more intimate
fervour. Nevertheless this fervour was largely intellectual, and he
did not throw his whole emotional being into the matter. But
here this is precisely what he does. The agonizings of Troilus are
subtle and intellectualized and yet quite pervaded by the mind's
full emotions:

> Within my soul there doth conduce a fight
> Of this strange nature that a thing inseparate
> Divides more wider than the sky and earth,
> And yet the spacious breadth of this division
> Admits no orifix for a point as subtle
> As Ariachne's broken woof to enter.

In writing on *Hamlet* I pointed out that the speech from which
this comes tells us the kind of emotional crisis Hamlet underwent

when his mother re-married in haste.* No one doubts the emotional intensity with which Shakespeare describes his disillusion. The same intensity will be readily allowed in Shakespeare's treatment of Troilus. How is it, then, that Troilus's agony, in itself the subject of poetry dangerously intenser than poetry elsewhere in the play, does not upset the total balance? First, because unlike Hamlet Troilus quickly gains mastery over feelings that threaten to break him. He ends his great speech by saying that the bits and greasy relics of Cressida's o'er-eaten faith are bound to Diomed. Ulysses interposes with

> May worthy Troilus be half attach'd
> With that which here his passion doth express?

This seems to mean 'May Troilus even with half his self be affected by the creature whose degradation he has just described?' Troilus with an unexpected twist of thought answers 'yes', but means it in a way Ulysses has not expected.

> Ay, Greek; and that shall be divulged well
> In characters as red as Mars his heart
> Inflamed with Venus. Never did young man fancy
> With so eternal and so fix'd a soul.
> Hark, Greek: as much as I do Cressid love,
> So much by weight hate I her Diomed.

Troilus is still the proverbial faithful lover, but that faithful love has been transmuted into a hatred of Diomed of equal measure and durability. Such a transmutation is at the other extreme from the protracted melancholy the same shock creates in Hamlet. It also cuts short those dangerous emotions, which, if allowed room, would have wrecked the rest of the play. Secondly, Troilus is never alone. Ulysses is there ready to prevent any violence against Cressida or Diomed and to help Troilus contain that storm of

* For a second parallel, this time from *Henry V*, and for possible personal applications of the kind of experience described, see Appendix D, p. 147.

nerves which might have broken out if he had been left to himself. Troilus protests his patience and just succeeds in honouring his protest; and when Aeneas enters he has regained his equipoise. 'Have with you, prince', he says to Aeneas; and to Ulysses, remembering his good offices, 'My courteous lord, adieu'. This wonderful scene, then, is all gain. It is a thrilling and unexpectedly rich culmination of one of the play's main themes and its richness does not compromise the play's prevailing tenor.

The rest of the play deals with the matter of Troy, as Shakespeare had committed himself to doing. It is not especially interesting but will bear comparison with the final battle scenes in *Macbeth*. I have already explained how the Hector of v. 3 who insists on going to fight, though restrained by wife, father, and sister, confirms the Hector of the Trojan council. The authenticity of the final scenes from v. 4 has been questioned; and on very insufficient grounds. Shakespeare was dealing with antique matter; he had the difficult task of showing in outline a big mass of sheer narrative. It is natural enough for him to be compressed and staccato or stylized. For instance, in describing how Achilles treacherously kills Hector, Shakespeare falls into his own early manner in *Henry VI*:

> Look, Hector, how the sun begins to set,
> How ugly night comes breathing at his heels.
> Even with the vail and darking of the sun,
> To close the day up, Hector's life is done.

Achilles's brutality reminds Shakespeare of the War of the Roses, where the decencies of chivalric warfare had been forgotten. If Shakespeare could archaize in the Hecuba passage in *Hamlet*, why not here? Further, Shakespeare maintains his characters throughout. It is the same Thersites. It is Ulysses and no one else who announces that the thing he had worked for all along has been achieved: the return of Achilles to battle. And it is his ally Nestor who adds just after, 'So, so, we draw together.' The difficulty of holding that a hack dramatist botching up the play could have made Nestor drop those words is in itself greater than all the difficulties that have been found in crediting these last scenes to Shakespeare.

The last two scenes need close reading. An innovation is that the gods come in very prominently: Agamemnon, speaking of Hector, ends scene nine with

> If in his death the gods have us befriended,
> Great Troy is ours, and our sharp wars are ended.

And we are meant to think of the 'protractive trials of great Jove', the words applied by Agamemnon in the first council scene to the seven years of the war so far elapsed. Immediately after, in scene ten, Troilus takes up the theme of the gods. After telling of Achilles dragging Hector's body behind his chariot Troilus says,

> Frown on, you heavens, effect your rage with speed,
> Sit, gods, upon your thrones, and smite* at Troy!
> I say, at once let your brief plagues be mercy,
> And linger not our sure destructions on!

And when Aeneas chides him for alarming the army with these words, Troilus says Aeneas misinterprets. What Troilus must mean, therefore, is that he is ready for the worst that heaven can do, and if Troy is to fall let it be at once. I do not think that Shakespeare here staged a last-moment piece of piety to retrieve a play in which the gods figure hardly at all. His object is technical. Three years were to elapse before Troy was to fall, and Troilus (but only after prodigies of valour), Achilles, and Paris had to die first. Even Shakespeare could not crowd all this into a single play. So the issue is taken out of the hands of men and deposited conveniently in the laps of the gods. And with the change the play

---

* I adopt the emendation of *smite* for *smile*. A scribe or compositor could easily have put *smile* in instinctive contrast with *frown* in the line before.

can more decently close. But not till Troilus confirms the fierce and resolute temper in which he left the scene of Cressida's infidelity and Pandarus has come on again, the Bawd not Lord Pandarus, to remind us of the other main theme.

W. W. Lawrence calls *Troilus and Cressida* 'an experiment in the middle ground between comedy and tragedy in which experience often places us; nothing is settled clearly for good or ill'; and I should agree that like *Hamlet* it is a play of display rather than of ordering. It resembles both *Hamlet* and *Much Ado* in the way a main plan miscarries, the intended effect being reached by the agency of chance. Neither Hamlet's mouse-trap nor Claudius's despatch of Hamlet to England advances the contriver's plans; Beatrice's propulsion of Benedict to avenge Hero is superfluous through the accidental usefulness of Dogberry; Ulysses's masterly machinations for rousing Achilles are of no account, and what all this protraction of effort has failed to do the unexpected news of Patroclus's death achieves in a moment. The picture then is one in which human plans count for little and the sheer gestation of time and what it reveals count for much. On this topic I can quote from an excellent passage in an article on the play in the *Times Literary Supplement*.* The writer points out that Time here is not only a destroying or 'calumniating' power but 'a mysterious co-operator with the individual in bringing events to pass whose "thievish progress to eternity" must be stayed by seizing the value of the present moment'. The writer goes on to speak of the play's characters as follows:

> The characters do not dominate Time and, so to speak, force its pace. They rather combine with it and acquiesce in its movement. . . .
>
> The end crowns all
> And that old common arbitrator Time
> Will one day end it.

In the great tragedies Shakespeare has no use for a Time of that nature: in them man hurries events along on the swift tide of his will. But the

* 19 May 1932.

pace of tragic Time is too swift and strong for men not of the highest temper.

This is said of *Troilus and Cressida* but it applies to *Hamlet* as well. Both are primarily dramas where the sheer wealth of the display counts for more than the lessons we learn from the way events are disposed. For such lessons we do indeed require characters who force the pace, who make time run; if display is required, no matter if designs cancel out or come to nothing and characters are either weak or stopped from doing. The Trojan council scene resulted in no action at all but was highly successful in revealing the cross-currents of human motives. Troilus's love could never have its proper fruition in a rich activity of mind and deed because its object was unworthy; yet the sheer display of its striving and of its betrayal is sufficiently exciting and instructive. Ulysses's politics turn out to be superfluous in practice, yet how fascinating in themselves.

Of course, *Troilus and Cressida* is inferior to *Hamlet*. The verse, though wonderfully varied and fresh, lacks the surpassing thrill. And there is no implication of life beyond what is explicitly presented: nothing to correspond to Marcellus's description of the preparations for war. Further, in spite of Troilus's passions and sufferings when he witnesses Cressida's infidelity, the general temper is cooler and more critical. Hamlet may fail to force Time but he agonizes over his failure, and in so doing heightens the emotional temperature. In *Troilus and Cressida* the characters are not aware of their failure. Lastly, the religious temper of *Hamlet* makes it richer than the other play. In Ulysses's speech on Degree the angelic end of the chain of being is omitted; and this is typical of the whole of *Troilus and Cressida*. The human beings here provide their own background. In *Hamlet* the setting is nothing less than the whole universe. Nevertheless, though more restricted than *Hamlet*, *Troilus and Cressida* is a very fine drama of display and as such deserves a higher than its normal reputation.

Like *Hamlet* again *Troilus and Cressida* shows a powerful

intellectual grasp in the way events are disposed and characters manipulated. The one weakness is, as explained above, a possible inconsistency in the hero's character. But there are features that correspond to the masterly pattern in *Hamlet*, where certain motives are set forth in the first act and worked out with precise correspondence in the third. First, there is the cunning union of the two great themes: the love of Troilus and the war for Troy. Secondly, there is the emergence of Troilus and Ulysses as the dominant characters and the consequent subordination of the others to them. This emergence is a gradual process and it serves to give the play something like a plot and something which counteracts the more critical theme of motives miscarrying or being found superfluous.

But there is more yet in the dominance and contrast of these two characters, for they are more than their sole selves, standing for certain sides of life. Troilus, crudely, stands for Honour, and Ulysses for Policy; and as such they represent Trojans and Greeks. Further, the Trojans are antique, the Greek modern. Such an interpretation is not at all surprising. Shakespeare, I believe, had a livelier sense of history than is usually allowed. He had hinted at the decay of chivalry in the second and third parts of *Henry VI*. In *Richard II* the antique world, so full of colour but so inefficient, goes down before the new efficiency. In *All's Well*, as I shall point out, an old world, better than the young, is dying. Something of these contrasts is found in Shakespeare's Trojans and Greeks. The Trojans are the older chivalric aristocrats and they lack cunning. The Greeks are the new men; and though they are not very efficient and quarrel, at least Ulysses and Achilles have an eye to the main chance. They are not shackled by chivalric scruples; and Time, to which they are better attuned, is on their side. Finally – and this is pure conjecture not to be taken too seriously – may not the very persistent references to merchandise amount to something? Does Shakespeare associate the lowered tone of the play with the spread of the new commercialism, seeing in the Greeks the new commercial classes, not so very efficient but more so than the waning aristocracy? This is the kind of conjecture that I dislike; and this very dislike may slightly validate a notion which insisted on forming itself while I was studying the play.

Finally, it cannot be asserted too strongly that Shakespeare in writing *Troilus and Cressida* did not alter his moral standards. The old interpretation of the play as an outburst of unrestrained bitterness against life, to be overcome later, is fantastically false. Hector is honourable and generous and he fails to apply his virtues to real life: but that does not mean that Shakespeare temporarily despised honour and generosity. Cressida is shallow, hard, and lascivious. Had Shakespeare been really bitter, he would have been glad to see her making Troilus suffer. But he is not in the least glad. The same ethical standards prevail as in the rest of Shakespeare; and far from imposing his opinions on us, Thersites has his own foul interpretation of others, cast back on himself. On the other hand Shakespeare did, in this play, choose to show things happening rather than men so making things happen as to imply a clear and powerful moral scheme. But things *can* happen in the way he presents them; here is an undoubted (though by no means the only) aspect of experience. To present such an aspect rather than to order experience does not show that a man denies all possibility of an order. When he wrote *Troilus and Cressida* Shakespeare was a popular dramatist with work to his credit already very well known. To isolate the play from Shakespeare's total moral context up to that date is to violate the conditions in which he wrote it.

Shakespeare's presentation of a certain side of experience has its own proper fascination. Exploiting a range of feelings more critical and sophisticated than elemental and unfeignedly passionate, he can play with language, spring surprises on us, mingle pathos and satire, play with the fire of tragedy without getting burnt and end by leaving us guessing. If we accept it that he meant to leave us guessing, and if we allow that the material and the tradition he inherited forced him to accept a slightly bigger burden than he could bear, we can make all necessary allowances and can end in finding in *Troilus and Cressida* a powerful if astringent delight.

Notes on *Troilus and Cressida*

I had thought that my segregation of Troilus and Ulysses as the two main characters and my depreciation of Hector's chivalric nobility were new and hence the more likely to give offence. But I find that Dowden has anticipated this opinion in the preface to his third edition of *Shakspere, his Mind and Art*. There he makes Troilus and Ulysses counterparts, recognizes that Troilus is of tough fibre and emerges a man, calls Hector 'heroic but too careless how and when he expends his heroic strength' and classes him with Ajax and Achilles as 'of minor importance'. I am glad to have such support in a contention which affects the whole lay-out of the play.

I have not referred to Heywood, *The Iron Age*, because I agree with those who date it after *Troilus and Cressida* (see especially E. K. Chambers, *William Shakespeare*, I, p. 449).

I am glad to have the support of W. B. D. Henderson in my opinion that Shakespeare owed a lot to Lydgate (Parrott Presentation Volume, Princeton, 1935, p. 128).

I must repeat that I am indebted to what W. W. Lawrence and Oscar Campbell have written on the play. In Lawrence's article, 'Troilus, Cressida and Thersites,' in *Modern Language Review*, 1942, pp. 422–37, there is an excellent passage (p. 427) about Shakespeare's 'leaving his audience to draw their own conclusions, just as each man constructs his philosophy of life out of his own experience' and (p. 429) a cogent refutation of some of Oscar Campbell's contentions. I think Lawrence exaggerates the play's violences and broad coarse effects. I must record my debt to Wolfgang Keller's sane and considered but rather conventional account of the play in *Shakespear-Jahrbuch*, 1930, pp. 182–207; to Olwen W. Campbell's acute and lively article in *London Mercury*, 1921, pp. 48–59 (though I disagree with her about Hector); and to Theodore Spencer's passage on the play in *Shakespeare and the Nature of Man*, New York, 1942, pp. 109–21.

Finally, there is Una Ellis-Fermor's interpretation of *Troilus and Cressida* in the *Frontiers of Drama* (London, 1945), pp. 56–76. She asserts that Shakespeare did really express a conviction of chaos, but unconsciously countered by a sense of order implicit in the artistic form. This is an interesting psychological interpretation, but I find that it makes the play less consciously critical in tone and more abandoned in its passions than I am prepared to make it.

ALL'S WELL THAT ENDS WELL

IT is agreed that *All's Well* is in some sort a failure. But there are many kinds of failure, some dull, some interesting, some tame, some heroic, some simple, some complicated. The failure of *All's Well* is not indeed heroic, like that of *Measure for Measure,* but it is interesting and it is complicated: well worth the attempt to define.

But perhaps it is premature to talk of failure. Fail the play does, when read: but who of its judges have seen it acted? Not I at any rate; and I suspect that it acts far better than it reads. For one thing it is very well plotted; and in the usual Shakespearean manner. The main outlines of the opening position are set forth quickly and emphatically in the first act. We learn what has just happened at Rossillion, the natures of the chief characters, and the main-spring of the whole action, Helena's passion for Bertram. That passion drives her to Paris to try her luck; and the second act mounts to a swift climax in the two long scenes where Helena first persuades the French King to try her remedy and then claims her reward in the hand of Bertram, only to gain the show and not the substance of her wishes. The middle of the play, as so often in Shakespeare, is filled with preparatory action rather than fruition, with the process of incubation not of birth. But this process proceeds with firm logic from the more crowded and open events of the first two acts. In Florence, in the fourth act, events again thicken and gather speed. They culminate in the long third scene, which takes place at night. Here Bertram is assailed by one surprise or excitement after another. He receives a very disturbing letter from his mother, he hears of the French King's strong resentment at some of his actions, he thinks that he has triumphed in his illicit courtship of Diana, only to have his relationship with her altered and endangered by the supposed news that his wife is dead, and he finds he has been deceived in his friend and adviser Parolles. But he does not know the full truth, namely that his wife is alive and had substituted herself for Diana that very night. The last act works out all the things that result from the full truth's being revealed.

This admirable construction, which I cannot remember to have seen sufficiently praised, might be more evident on the stage than in the study and might ensure for the play a position far higher than its present one, should it ever force its way into the repertory that enjoys regular presentation. But on the only available criterion, that of reading, it remains true that in its total effect *All's Well* fails and that the failure is caused most obviously by the comparative feebleness of execution. This is not to deny the skill in plotting, but the effect and the virtue of plotting vary according to the success of other parts of a composition. If I may quote something I wrote before:

The virtue of the plot only begins when other qualities are already there. Many modern detective stories are ephemeral in spite of excellent plotting. . . . But that does not mean that plot is never important. Easy though it is for a cool self-possessed mind to plot ingeniously, it becomes a matter of greater difficulty and greater importance when the imagination grows hot. The cool brain has no temptations not to plot well, but without these temptations plotting well amounts to nothing.*

And the trouble with *All's Well* is that though Shakespeare's imagination does grow warm at times and at a few points genuinely incandescent, there is no steady warmth pervading the whole creation. And this lack of imaginative warmth shows in a

* E. M. W. Tillyard, *Poetry Direct and Oblique* (revised edition, London, 1945), pp. 75–6.

defective poetical style. I will quote two examples of Shakespeare's imagination half-kindled but only half and hence not succeeding. The first is from the play's first scene and is spoken by Helena of Parolles, after she has soliloquized on her love for Bertram and when she sees Parolles approaching:

> Who comes here?
> One that goes with him. I love him for his sake,
> And yet I know him a notorious liar,
> Think him a great way fool, solely a coward.
> Yet these fixt evils sit so fit in him
> That they take place, when virtue's steely bones
> Look bleak i' th' cold wind. Withal, full oft we see
> Cold wisdom waiting on superfluous folly.

These lines act on us as Chapman often does. They raise high expectations, creating a promising sense of afflatus, and yet fail to fulfil them. There is something very striking about virtue's steely bones looking bleak in the cold wind, but what strikes initially is an irrelevant image: bones or a skeleton in the open blown on by the winds of heaven:

> O'er his white banes, when they are bare,
> The wind sall blaw for evermair.

But Virtue is pictured as a person and not as a skeleton; so we have to correct and, when we do so, we do not get an immediate and undoubted image. We may first think of a thin haggard face with prominent cheek-bones and jaw; but such faces look bleak whether exposed to the cold air or not: there is little propriety in the thought. Finally, we may argue back from cold, that is naked, wisdom waiting on superfluous, that is overdressed, folly and conclude that Virtue is a naked wretch excluded from a firm place in society while Vices are received. But even so the picture hardly exists: the imagination is hardly stirred; and we must conclude that the author's imagination too was not properly kindled.

The second passage is spoken by Helena after Bertram, un-knowing, has begotten his child on her:

> But O strange men,
> That can such sweet use make of what they hate,
> When saucy trusting of the cozen'd thoughts
> Defiles the pitchy night: so lust doth play
> With what it loathes for that which is away.
>
> (IV. 4. 21–5)

This, roughly, means: how strange men are in being able to get such pleasure from and give such pleasure to the person they hate, when a proneness, bred of wanton thoughts, to be deluded more than matches in its moral darkness the actual darkness of night. So it happens that lust enjoys the object of its hate in place of the absent object of its desire. The first line and a half are perfect, simple in expression yet striking in effect, conveying much in little. But the next line and a half are obscure and clotted, yielding their sense to the intellect rather than to the imagination, creating no lively image; they are strange, but barrenly so. The defects show up at once when set beside the lines of *Measure for Measure* which, dealing with the same subject, Claudio's intercourse with Juliet, and using the same words, *saucy* and *sweet*, cannot be independent of the present passage. Here Angelo, commenting on this intercourse, says:

> Ha, fie, these filthy vices! It were as good
> To pardon him that hath from nature stolen
> A man already made as to remit
> Their saucy sweetness that do coin heaven's image
> In stamps that are forbid.
>
> (II. 4. 42–6)

Here all is brilliantly clear and pointed, and the imagery can be dwelt on with advantage. Murder is a theft from nature and is likened to the theft of gold: than such theft forging illicit coin is no better. But begetting an illegitimate child is just such forgery;

hence no better than murder. Helena's words indeed 'defile the pitchy night' in comparison with this clarity.

This failure of the poetic imagination in these two passages typifies a general failure throughout the play. The construction is, as already noted, masterly and so is the way the characters are outlined; and these ensure great interest for the play: but the execution, lacking the supreme imaginative warmth, fails to bring these great virtues to fruition. We shall never know the reason for this failure, which may well have been nothing more complicated than an attack of the toothache at the critical time of creation; but it may help a little to point out that Shakespeare had, in the plot he chose and in the treatment he proposed to give it, set himself a task of great difficulty.

One of Shakespeare's recurrent problems as a comedy writer was how to combine the romantic and improbable and fantastic plots he usually chose with a vitality and a realism of characterization which his own inclinations insisted on. He had more than one solution. For instance, in *Much Ado* he puts his realism into the sub-plots: the persons in the so-called main plot, Claudio, Hero, Don John, are so little characterized that they pass well enough in their improbable setting. In the *Merchant of Venice* the most realistic and highly developed character is Shylock and he threatens through his overdevelopment to upset the fairy-tale world to which in his original capacity of Big Bad Man he was appropriate. Shakespeare maintains the harmony, or rather creates a richer one, by bringing out the Jewish character of the real world Shylock inhabits: for Jewish meant strange and alien; and this strangeness is the connecting link with the different strangeness of the world of the fairy-tale. In *All's Well*, as W. W. Lawrence has brought out so admirably, the main material is from folk-lore. It comprises two different but immemorial folk themes: the healing of a king leading to marriage and the fulfilment of certain seemingly impossible tasks. Shakespeare in choosing such material and then in making the main characters concerned, the

French King, Bertram, and Helena, highly realistic set himself a problem of the first difficulty, far harder than those in the *Merchant of Venice* and *Much Ado*, only to be solved by the application of his highest powers. Consider these three characters for a moment. Of these the French King is the most sketchily drawn, yet set him beside some of the other royal persons in mature Shakespearean comedy and see the result. Orsino is lover rather than ruler and is hardly comparable. But take Don Pedro from *Much Ado* and the two Dukes in *As You Like It*, consider what flat figures these are, and then notice the relative realism of the French King, with his tiredness, his strong sense of duty, his warm-hearted loyalty to his newly dead friend, Bertram's father, his distrust of the steadiness of the younger generation, and his noble yet pathetic anxiety not to outlast his usefulness. 'Would I were with him!' is his comment to Bertram on his dead father:

> Would I were with him! He would always say –
> Methinks I hear him now – his plausive words
> He scatter'd not in ears but grafted them
> To grow there and to bear: 'Let me not live' –
> This his good melancholy oft began
> On the catastrophe and heel of pastime
> When it was out – 'Let me not live', quoth he,
> 'After my flame lacks oil, to be the snuff
> Of younger spirits, whose apprehensive senses
> All but new things disdain, whose judgments are
> Mere feathers of their garments, whose constancies
> Expire before their fashions.' This he wish'd.
> I, after him, do after him wish too,
> Since I nor wax nor honey can bring home,
> I quickly were dissolved from my hive
> To give some labourers room.
>
> (I. 2. 52-67)

There you have living characterization, recalling the portrayal of Henry IV more than that of the comedy princes. Bertram, again, is a far more detailed study than the Claudios and Antonios and Orlandos of the genuine comedies; a character drawn from a close and not very friendly study of spoilt and unlicked aristocracy. Helena, too, is far closer to actual life than the heroine, psychologically untroubled, charming and witty, usual in the comedies, and reminds one rather of the troubled psyche of Euripides's Electra. Now Shakespeare was really interested in such characterization when he wrote *All's Well*; and we know it because the play's freest poetry goes to establish it – witness the French King's speech just quoted. All the greater therefore was his difficulty in dealing with folk-lore material where psychological subtlety is least to the point.

It is interesting to compare Shakespeare with his original and to see how Boccaccio coped with his inherited fairy-tale material. Boccaccio's problem was similar: he had to tame the fabulous into the realistic and the sophisticated. But he set himself a less exacting standard of realism: all he aimed at was a diverting story that would not overtax the powers of a lively and critical audience to suspend willingly their disbelief. So he contented himself with keeping the characters simple, with inserting a few realistic touches like Helena's efficient management of Bertram's estate while he is in Italy, and with taking the fabulous lightly. Above all he has that supreme confidence of the great artist really in control of his material enabling him to tell his story, fabulous though it may be, in a simple and compelling way that leaves the reader no option but unqualified acceptance. He allows his reader no more doubt than Dostoevski when he describes the monastery at the beginning of the *Brothers Karamazov*. All this is remote from Shakespeare both as regards the task set and the way it is carried out.

Such then are some of the ways in which Shakespeare failed as a whole and incidentally some of the ways in which he scored partial successes. Before passing to what Shakespeare did achieve I must speak of some of the subsidiary problems that confront any critic of the play.

Some of these problems have been thoroughly disposed of by W. W. Lawrence. For instance, he makes it clear that, by the rules of the game Shakespeare was playing, our sympathies are meant to be with Helena. Such a contention is important, and it warns us to be careful of sympathizing overmuch with Bertram in what appears to a modern a wickedly cruel situation. By modern standards the King acts very hardly to Bertram in forcing Helena upon him. We are too apt to explain this hardness as something forced on the King by his oath. Doubtless some such motive is required but not to the extent usually thought necessary. For, by Elizabethan standards, the King is less hard than by ours. Bertram was his ward, and at his disposal. Helena was beautiful and intelligent, a fit bride for any young nobleman apart from her birth. And when the King says,

> 'Tis only title thou disdain'st in her, the which
> I can build up,

an Elizabethan audience would have accepted the plea and have considered Bertram to have had as fair a deal as the way of the world made usual.

Another problem that Lawrence seeks to settle is the modern resentment at the theme of the substitute bride, or the bed-trick, as it is sometimes called. He argues that this was a traditional motive, familiar to the audience, a piece of fairy-lore that could be accepted without question. Here, however, I doubt if the matter can be settled so simply. The popular opinion against the bed-trick here and in *Measure for Measure* has been too strong to be disregarded or explained away. It is a safe rule that you should always respect popular opinion or apparent prejudice and always suspect the reasons alleged for it. And, as a preliminary, it may be useful to ask why popular opinion has objected to the bed-trick and not objected to something in itself equally disgusting in

Twelfth Night, namely Olivia's accepting Sebastian as a substitute lover for Cesario. The idea that Viola and Sebastian had interchangeable souls is a monstrous insult to human nature. Yet it is a convention which in the play popular opinion has had no difficulty in accepting. The conclusion seems to be that convention by itself is not enough to secure acceptance: the context has to be taken into account. Now in *Measure for Measure* the context is of that seriousness that the fairy-lore of the bed-trick is somehow shocking, and popular opinion has rightly been hostile. On the other hand this hostility has been wrongly extended to the same incident in *All's Well*. For all the realism of the characters, the moral earnestness of *All's Well* never approaches that of *Measure for Measure*. We remain in a moral climate where incidents may happen unquestioned and where convention can evade scrutiny. We are vaguely on Helena's side and we wish her well in her intrinsically dubious adventure.

Yet another problem concerns certain passages which some critics have found strange or unworthy of Shakespeare and which they have explained as being either not Shakespeare at all or relics of much earlier work.* There are many such passages and I deal only with the longer. The first is the talk between Helena and Parolles near the opening of the play (I. I. 117) on virginity. It is in part both feeble and indecent, and critics have sought to relieve Shakespeare of it and give it to a collaborator or interpolator. But is there any proof? The episode is not mere accretion. Parolles is an important character, at once the corrupter of Bertram and the excuse for his ill practices; and we need to make his acquaintance early in the play. Part of the feeble volubility of the wit may be dramatic: Parolles must be voluble to live up to his name. And as for the actual writing being unworthy of Shakespeare, he had written this kind of rhetoric, for set rhetoric it is.

---

* For more detailed treatment of supposed 'stratification' in *All's Well* see Appendix E, p. 149.

more than once before. Take first some of the sentences on virginity:

PAROLLES: There's little that can be said in't, 'tis against the rule of nature. To speak on the part of virginity is to accuse your mothers, which is most infallible disobedience. He that hangs himself is a virgin: virginity murders itself and should be buried in highways out of all sanctified limit, as a desperate offendress against nature. Virginity breeds mites, much like a cheese; consumes itself to the very paring and so dies with feeding his own stomach. Besides, virginity is peevish, proud, idle, made of self-love, which is the most inhibited sin in the canon. Keep it not: you cannot choose but lose by it; out with it.

Parolles does not speak so well on virginity as Falstaff does on honour, but their words belong to the same author. Or take the following passage on conscience:

I'll not meddle with it. It makes a man a coward: a man cannot steal but it accuseth him; a man cannot swear but it checks him; a man cannot lie with his neighbour's wife but it detects him. 'Tis a blushing shamefast spirit that mutinies in a man's bosom; it fills a man full of obstacles: it made me once restore a purse of gold that by chance I found; it beggars any man that keeps it. It is turned out of all towns and cities for a dangerous thing; and every man that means to live well endeavours to trust to himself and live without it.

This is Clarence's Second Murderer in *Richard III* speaking and he treats conscience just as Parolles treats virginity, enumerating the different crimes the quality is guilty of and referring to scripture through the Ten Commandments where Parolles does so through parodying St Paul on charity. Since Shakespeare had written already at least twice in this vein, why seek to deprive him of a third manifestation? And as to the ineptitude of Helena joining in the talk, that is prepared for by her comment on Parolles as he enters to the effect that she knows him to be a liar, a fool, and a coward but that she loves him because he is Bertram's companion. Parolles, speaking in the vicarious glamour of Bertram, can be tolerated, however nasty or windy his talk.

Then there are the couplets; and it is true that these are many and that some occur in places where they are least expected in Shakespeare's mature work. The most conspicuous places are in the second act. In II. 1. 133, when Helena makes her final and successful attempt to persuade the King to try her remedy, blank verse gives place to couplets; and in II. 3. 78 Helena, having spoken mature and lovely blank verse before making her actual choice of a husband, falls into the stiffness and ceremony of rhyme. This use of rhyme at the high moments of action is indeed extraordinary. But it is not unparalleled in Shakespeare, for exactly the same thing happens in the *First Part of Henry VI* where Talbot and his son perish in couplets. But though the parallel may argue for the authenticity of the couplets in *All's Well*, the question remains why he chose to use them in such places. In my answer to it the matter of 'stratification' may come up at the same time, but it is in itself subsidiary; for if Shakespeare chose to use chunks of earlier work these must be considered no less organic to his scheme than the actual insects or postage stamps or leaves gummed on to the canvas of a surrealist picture.

In the conversation between Helena and the King it is the King who gives the cue with (line 133),

> Thou thought'st to help me; and such thanks I give
> As one near death to those that wish him live.

But Helena takes up the cue and has most of the talk to the end of the scene. What is most evident in her first speeches is their piety and their suggestion of a miracle:

> He that of greatest works is finisher
> Oft does them by the weakest minister.
> So holy writ in babes hath judgement shown,
> When judges have been babes; great floods have flown
> From simple sources and great seas have dried,
> When miracles have by the greatest been denied.

The 'baby judges' could be Daniel judging Susanna, or the wise

'babes and sucklings' of the Gospels. The 'flood' is the water
struck from the rock by Moses at Horeb and Kadesh; the sea is
the Red Sea as described in Exodus. In her second speech Helena
continues in the same strain in answer to the King's doubts:

> Inspired merit so by breath is barr'd.
> It is not so with Him that all things knows
> As 'tis with us that square our guess by shows.
> But most it is presumption in us when
> The help of heaven we count the act of men.
> Dear sir, to my endeavours give consent;
> Of heaven, not me, make an experiment.

Here again there is scriptural reference, in the first line; a general
reference to Hebrew kings who denied the truth of the inspired
prophets. This accumulation of scriptural reference, this calling
in the help of God, and this confidence in a forthcoming miracle
combine to give a special character to this portion of the scene.
Shakespeare may have got his hint from his original, which runs
'The King, hearing these words, said to himself: "This woman
peradventure is sent unto me of God".' But, whether or not, he
surely must have used the pomp and stiffness of rhyme as appropriate to a solemn and hieratic content. The hieratic tone is continued in Helena's next speech, a speech habitually quoted as
obviously early work and as strong evidence for stratification.
To the King's question of how long the cure will take Helena
replies:

> The great'st grace lending grace,
> Ere twice the horses of the sun shall bring
> Their fiery torcher his diurnal ring,
> Ere twice in murk and occidental damp
> Moist Hesperus hath quench'd his sleepy lamp,
> Or four and twenty times the pilot's glass
> Hath told the thievish minutes how they pass,
> What is infirm from your sound parts shall fly,
> Health shall live free and sickness freely die.

Now though it is very queer that Shakespeare should write so tall at so crucial a place in the play, it is pretty plain what he is doing. He is deliberately evading drama and substituting ritual and cloudy incantation. And it makes matters more rather than less queer to postulate just here a theft from an old play or the calling in of a bad poet to do an inferior job of work. The resemblance of these lines to the beginning of the *Murder of Gonzago* in *Hamlet* has sometimes been noticed; and to some this resemblance indicates a collaborator still more strongly. To me it suggests that Shakespeare had at his call a rather clumsy and heightened style in rhyme which he used from time to time to mark certain passages in his plays violently off from the rest. Some such style was plainly needed for a play within a play: the need for its use in the scene under discussion is far from obvious, but, that need granted, the style itself should not cause us undue surprise or necessitate unusual explanations.

I maintain therefore that you need not invoke stratification or collaborators to help explain the play: first because they cannot explain the really puzzling things and secondly because what they can explain admits of other explanations. It is, on the other hand, impossible to disprove stratification or collaboration; and if I now dismiss the notion of them it is for reasons of probability not of verifiable truth.

I revert now to what I have principally noted of the play: Shakespeare's failure to kindle his imagination at the high places of the action. I have pointed out the difficulty, exceptional in his comedies, in which he involved himself: that of fitting a highly realistic set of principal actors into a plot belonging to the fantastic world of fairy-lore. And it is quite possible that this difficulty explains the imaginative failure: that Shakespeare, knowing when he came to actual composition that he could not succeed, evaded the attempt and resorted, when the crises came, to the conventional, the sentential, or the hieratic, never taxing his full imaginative powers. The very consistency makes this apparent evasion the more likely. There is no weight of evidence that Shakespeare changed his mind during composition. There is indeed one place where action and high poetry are combined: Helena's soliloquy after she has heard Bertram's refusal to return to France while his wife is there. She blames herself for the dangers he now undergoes in the Florentine wars and resolves to quit the country so that he may return:

> O you leaden messengers,
> That ride upon the violent speed of fire,
> Fly with false aim, move the still-piecing air,
> That sings with piercing; do not touch my lord.
> Whoever shoots at him, I set him there;
> Whoever charges on his forward breast,
> I am the caitiff that do hold him to't.
> And though I kill him not I am the cause
> His death was so effected. Better 'twere
> I met the ravin lion when he roar'd
> With sharp constraint of hunger; better 'twere
> That all the miseries which nature owes
> Were mine at once. No, come thou home, Rossillion,
> Whence honour but of danger wins a scar
> As oft it loses all. I will be gone:
> My being here it is that holds thee hence.
> Shall I stay here to do't? No, no, although
> The air of paradise did fan the house
> And angels offic'd all.

It is futile to ask why Shakespeare's imagination was here, uniquely, kindled. The present point is that such kindling is unique, that the high places of the action before and after fail to evoke high poetry, and that such failure remains the consistent rule. It looks as if Shakespeare, however ill-satisfied with what he was doing, at least knew it from the start and stuck to it.

Not that he stuck to the same method of writing below his stylistic height at the high places. As noted already, he makes

Helena speak heavy and involved couplets when at the end of the play's first scene she makes her great resolve to try her fortune in Paris, he makes Helena and the King speak strange and hieratic couplets when she persuades him to try her cure, and he makes Helena drop into couplets when she chooses her husband. Between this last scene (II. 3) and the scene (IV. 3) containing many nocturnal happenings and critical for Bertram there is no long emphatic scene. The intervening happenings are parcelled out into short scenes; action is competently described in a middle style, mature but in point of poetry not distinguished though better than the sententious or hieratic couplets. But the effect is to dissipate, to make the temperature of action warm not hot. Such dissipation was wise, for the critical scene which crowns the action (IV. 3) is nearly all in prose. It is in itself admirable, but its prose provides yet one more example of the means of depressing high action. The unmasking of Parolles could, of course, in any kind of treatment be only in prose, but the preliminary moral comments of the two French Lords on Bertram and Bertram's own mental crises could have lent themselves to high poetical treatment. The last scene of the play, when the whole truth comes out, again offered excellent chances of poetry. Shakespeare refuses or evades them, not (on the whole) by sententious couplet writing, nor by using prose instead of verse, but by sheer ingenuity and complication of plot. In Shakespeare's original, Giletta, having fulfilled her tasks, confronts Beltramo, who has returned home, on a feast day and makes good her claims simply and directly. Shakespeare could have imitated this simplicity, but he vastly complicates the action by the business of the rings and by making Diana and her mother travel to France. There is so much business and so many surprises that there is little room for the deeper feelings and hence no call for high poetry.

So far I have spoken mainly of what the play fails in and of how possibly it comes to do so. I pass on now to some of its positive qualities.

Though we need not impute bitterness or cynicism to the general complexion of the play, we cannot but find it full of suffering. And the sense of suffering is heightened because there are hints of an earlier prosperity which the final reconciliation of Bertram and Helena does not promise to equal. The earlier prosperity is detected through the aged characters. The Countess resembles the old lady on whom William Empson wrote one of his best poems. She is 'ripe', full of experience and with wide and generous sympathies; but she is also a 'cooling planet' and the crops she reaps though in her sole control are scanty. Her husband had been a spendid person, and Rossillion in his day must have had other and gayer representatives than his 'unbaked and doughy' son, his taut-nerved physician's daughter, and the 'shrewd and unhappy fool' whom his widow keeps in her service out of kindness and respect for her husband's memory. The French King had evidently been all that a king should be, but now he 'nor wax nor honey can bring home'. And even after Helena has cured him he regains no joy in life. He conducts his examination of Bertram in the last act efficiently enough, but his chief vitality goes to fostering his (very natural) suspicions that Bertram has murdered Helena:

> My fore-past proofs, howe'er the matter fall,
> Shall tax my fears of little vanity,
> Having vainly fear'd too little. . . .
> I am wrapp'd in dismal thinkings.

And even in the efficient exercise of his duties is insinuated the fact of his age:

> Let's take the instant by the forward top;
> For we are old, and on our quick'st decrees
> The inaudible and noiseless foot of time
> Steals, ere we can effect them.

Lafeu indeed has plenty of vitality, as when he calls his desponding master 'my royal fox' and asks him if he will eat no grapes and when he detects the fraud of Parolles. Yet we know all the time he is old:

Iam senior, sed cruda *viro* viridisque senectus.

In front of these memories or relics of past happiness and vigour are set the hungry and unsatisfied or dour representatives of the present generation: the boorish and unlicked aristocrat Bertram, the Clown who hates being one, the two adventurers, one good the other contemptible, Helena and Parolles, Diana, correct but uneasy through poverty and a widowed mother, and the two French Lords, faintly drawn perhaps but correct rather than gay, and severely orthodox and even theological in their talk. The whole presentation is wonderfully interesting, and the closeness to actual life of some of the characters is remarkable. Yet the world these characters inhabit is cold and forbidding. We get no feeling, as we do in *Hamlet*, of varied life being transacted along with the happenings proper to the play itself. The sense of incompleteness noticed in the poetry of two short passages hangs over the whole play. The imagination has not done its full work. The artistic process has somehow halted before completion. Of all poets Shakespeare is least prone to violate the drama by speaking in his own person. Yet here there is the suspicion that his personal feelings, unobjectified and untransmuted, have slipped illegitimately into places which his poetic imagination, not fully kindled, has not succeeded in reaching. The evident dislike of the younger generation, for instance, has got a slight touch of the personal in it, as if, at that time, Shakespeare did actually compare it, to its disadvantage, with a more settled and more gracious age, now expiring and ineffective.

For the pious and theological tone, the conversation between the French King and Helena, when she persuades him to try her cure, has already been cited. It is of heaven, not of Helena, that the King makes experiment; and his cure is miraculous, not only as proclaimed by Helena, but, when effected, as reported by Lafeu:

They say miracles are past; and we have our philosophical persons, to make modern and familiar, things supernatural and causeless. Hence is it that we make trifles of terrors, ensconcing ourselves into seeming knowledge, when we should submit ourselves to an unknown fear. . . . A showing of a heavenly effect in an earthly actor. . . . The very hand of heaven.

Nor does the conception of Helena as a person specially favoured by heaven cease with her curing the King. The Countess, hearing Bertram has cast her away, says

> What angel shall
> Bless this unworthy husband? he cannot thrive,
> Unless her prayers, whom heaven delights to hear
> And loves to grant, reprieve him from the wrath
> Of greatest justice.

Nor does Shakespeare let the theme of Helena's divine agency drop. In IV. 4 she says to Diana's mother

> Doubt not but heaven
> Hath brought me up to be your daughter's dower,
> As it hath fated her to be my motive
> And helper to a husband.

But the most explicitly theological place in the play is the beginning of the culminating scene, IV. 3, where the two French Lords comment on Bertram's conduct. Not only the position but the speakers make this comment important. The two French Lords are the choric characters, the *punctum indifferens* of the play, and what they say gives a standard to which the play itself can be referred. After the First Lord has recounted, with strong disapproval, Bertram's seduction of Diana, these words follow :*

SECOND LORD: Now God lay our rebellion! As we are ourselves, what things are we.

FIRST LORD: Merely our own traitors. And as in the common course of

* I adopt Dover Wilson's assignment of the speeches to the two Lords and his emendation of *lay* for *delay* at the beginning.

all treasons, we still see them reveal themselves, till they attain to their abhorred ends; so he that in this action contrives against his own nobility in his proper stream o'erflows himself.

SECOND LORD: It is not meant damnable in us to be trumpeters of our unlawful intents?

There are two doctrines here: first and most emphatic, the theological doctrine of man's depravity unaided by divine grace, second, the doctrine that great crime will out, and often by the criminal giving himself away, to his ultimate punishment. Bertram, in his acts, has shown himself to be man cut off from grace, and by his indiscreet confidences, his 'o'erflowing himself', has prepared his own detection and punishment.

It looks, therefore, as if Shakespeare not only made Helena and Bertram highly realistic figures but made them represent heavenly grace and natural, unredeemed, man respectively. In fact, he had in his mind, possibly, the Spenserian practice of multiple meanings with so obvious an analogy as Britomart, who is at once a realistic character, a fiercely monogamous and jealous woman, and an allegorical representation of chastity; and, more likely, the Morality Play. And as in *Henry IV* there has been detected the Morality theme of man or the prince fought over by the virtues and vices (represented by Prince Hal, the Lord Chief Justice, and Falstaff); so here there are signs (not very emphatic) of the same theme. Bertram, as natural man, corresponds to Hal, the Prince; Helena corresponds to Honour and Justice as represented by the Lord Chief Justice; and Parolles, as often noted, corresponds to Falstaff. But I am far from wanting to press these correspondences; and it is nearer the truth to say that a second version of the Morality theme can be detected in *All's Well* than that Bertram copies Hal and Parolles Falstaff. Alexander* has rightly warned us not to press Johnson's remark that 'Parolles has many of the lineaments of Falstaff' too far, and rightly insists that 'Falstaff for all his vices belongs to another order of charac-

* *Op. cit.*, pp. 192-3.

ter'. Further, the Morality role of the tempter protrudes more obviously from the slight character of Parolles than from Falstaff's massiveness. In the same way Prince Hal, with his strong intellect, his wide knowledge of men, his irony, and his fundamental sense of duty, is remote from the unsophisticated and boorish Bertram. Moreover the relations between Prince Hal and Falstaff on the one hand and Bertram and Parolles on the other are totally different. Prince Hal knows what he is doing and has summed up Falstaff; it is Falstaff who is self-deceived about his influence on the Prince. Bertram is the simple dupe of Parolles's pretensions.

To detect the Morality motive in *All's Well* may be to add a new fact to the nature of the play; it does little to explain its character, for it is not strong enough to make itself powerfully felt. If Shakespeare had made the Morality motive very obvious and at the same time furnished it with his highly realistic characters, he might have done for Elizabethan drama what Euripides did for the Greek. This is not to say that Shakespeare copied the Morality perversely and without reason. In his last plays he was largely concerned with adjusting symbolism and real life; and only in the *Winter's Tale* and the *Tempest* did he succeed. It is perfectly natural that he should have made analogous experiments earlier in his career. Such an experiment I believe we have in *All's Well*.

I come now finally to the characters; and it is in the delineation of the main characters joined with the solid merit of the plot that the play's virtue most consists.

Of the three main characters – and they correspond to the Morality motive – least need be said about Parolles. Ever since Charles I substituted *Parolles* for *All's Well* as the play's title in his copy of the Second Folio, readers have recognized Parolles as a successful comic figure. He is a small impostor, but he puts up a tolerable show. His sermon on virginity to Helena is genuinely voluble; and he has a genuine if limited talent in imitating the language of his social superiors and claiming a knowledge of their manners. This talent comes out in the excellent comic passage (II. 1. 24–61) where Bertram laments to the two Lords and Parolles that he has been forbidden the wars:

> Noble heroes, my sword and yours are kin. Good sparks and lustrous, a word, good metals. You shall find in the regiment of the Spinii one Captain Spurio with his cicatrice, an emblem of war, here on his sinister cheek. It was this very sword entrenched it.

And when the Lords have gone and Bertram has been unable in the courtesy of farewell to squeeze out more than the ridiculous 'I grow to you, and our parting is a tortured body', Parolles shows some talent in his confirming his hold on Bertram with

> Use a more spacious ceremony to the noble lords. You have restrained yourself within the list of too cold an adieu. Be more expressive to them; for they wear themselves in the cap of the time, there do muster true gait, eat, speak, and move under the influence of the most received star: and, though the devil lead the measure, such are to be followed. After them, and take a more dilated farewell.

That is quite good imitation of the Rosencrantz and Guildenstern stuff; and it is not surprising that it needed the superior penetration of Lafeu to detect the fraud.

Critics have been too apt to exalt Helena at the expense of the other characters. She is no more interesting or instructive than Bertram; and the measure of neither character can be taken apart from the other. Nor is Van Doren right in saying that they both 'thin into a mere figure of fable as the plot wears on'. We learn indeed little new about Helena after she has put on her pilgrim's habit, but the crises through which Bertram passes in the last half of the play at once form the gist of the plot and reveal his nature. But though I disagree with Van Doren in this and in his centring all the 'blazing brightness of the play' in her, he has succeeded better than other critics in defining her character. Here are some of his remarks:

One of her favourite words is 'nature', and there is much of it in her. She has body as well as mind, and can jest grossly with Parolles. . . . There is nothing frail about Helena, whose passion is secret but unmeasured. And because her body is real her mind is gifted with a rank, a sometimes masculine fertility. It is easy for her to achieve the intellectual distinction of,

> 'In his bright radiance and collateral light'

just as it is natural that she should dress her longing for Bertram in the tough language of physics and metaphysics. . . . She has in her own dark way the force of Imogen, though she inhabits an inferior play.*

Van Doren is right. There is a formidable tautness in Helena's passion, which allies her with Spenser's Britomart, who, riding to rescue her lover Artegal from the Amazon Radegund, looked right down to hide the fellness of her heart, or to Susan, the fiercely monogamous woman in Virginia's Woolf's *The Waves*, who says that her love is fell. Rosalind and Viola are indeed in love but not with the strained passion of Helena. They say nothing to match, for instance, those lines she speaks, just before her open avowal of love, in answer to the Countess's protest 'I say, I am your mother';

> Pardon, madam;
> The Count Rossillion cannot be my brother.
> I am from humble, he from honour'd name;
> No note upon my parents, his all noble.
> My master, my dear lord he is; and I
> His servant live, and will his vassal die.
> He must not be my brother –

nor her words just before she chooses Bertram as her husband from the King's wards:

> The blushes in my cheeks thus whisper me,
> 'We blush that thou shouldst choose; but, be refused,

* *Op. cit.*, pp. 215–16.

> Let the white death sit on thy cheek for ever;
> We'll ne'er come there again.'

Not that Shakespeare makes her a mere humour of predatory monogamy. Twice her nerve fails her momentarily: first, when, like Isabella pleading with Angelo, she accepts the French King's first rebuff and nearly gives up; and second, when, having chosen and finding Bertram unwilling, she begs the King not to force the wedding. Such touches make us remember the terrible ordeal Helena had set herself: not to have quailed would argue her less or more than human. A further natural touch is her self-knowledge. Her strong intelligence does not spare her own self; as when she admits to the Countess that her resolve to cure the French King was not disinterested and that she would not have thought of it but for Bertram's journey to Paris. Nor has she the least illusion about Bertram's disposition.

The irony and the truth of Helena's situation are that with so much intelligence and so firm a mind she can be possessed by so enslaving a passion for an unformed, rather stupid, morally timid, and very self-centred youth: for by the standards of real life there is nothing surprising in Helena's having fallen for Bertram's handsome outside, his high rank, and her unconscious knowledge that she could dominate him and give him moral backbone, granted the chance. What is surprising is to see such truth of actual motivation, and one so little related to conventional motivation, figuring in an Elizabethan play.

For Bertram himself we must remember that the fight was not between himself and Helena. Helena had powerful allies, while he had only Parolles. The play's action is largely the story of how he yields to the pressure of numbers. But before pointing to that story, which as far as I know has not been clearly detected, I must substantiate some of the qualities I have given his character and indicate others.

In that list of qualities I did not include 'vicious'; and it is a triumph of art that Bertram can do so many selfish or mean things

without incurring that epithet. Though never more than natural
man, he is never, we feel, beyond the reach of grace. And that
Shakespeare just then appeared to rate natural man decidedly low
does not alter the fact. He keeps Bertram from positive vicious-
ness by asserting from the first, and then reiterating, his crude
immaturity. His mother, taking leave of Bertram in the first scene,
hopes he will 'succeed his father in manners as in shape', and
then adds ' 'Tis an unseason'd courtier' – which suggests that her
hope is far from certainty. The French King, on first seeing
Bertram, echoes the Countess's parting words

> Youth, thou bear'st thy father's face;
> Frank nature, rather curious than in haste,
> Hath well compos'd thee. Thy father's moral parts
> Mayst thou inherit too!

and goes on to praise Bertram's father in detail and to dispraise
the present generation of young men. Bertram's father 'looked
into the service of the time', that is had keen insight into military
affairs, and 'was discipled of the bravest', in other words was glad
to learn from his betters. Knowing that Bertram was under the
discipline of Parolles, we can infer his shortcomings easily enough
and the lubberly sense of guilt he must have felt when compared
with his elders and betters. Thereafter (quite apart from the
scanty and abrupt and sometimes boorish tone of Bertram's
speeches) the theme of his immaturity is maintained, for instance
through Lafeu's remark just before Helena chooses him for
husband, 'There's one grape yet, I am sure thy father drank wine:
but if thou be'st not an ass, I am a youth of fourteen; I have known
thee already', and through his later remark (beginning of IV. 5)
including Bertram among the 'unbaked and doughy youth of a
nation'. There is something pathetic as well as disagreeable in
Bertram's gruff and inhibited bearing. Hardly ever has he the
confidence to speak freely. He does so once when, in unguarded
fury at the proposed marriage, he disputes the King's command:

KING: Thou know'st she has rais'd me from my sickly bed.
BERTRAM: But follows it, my lord, to bring me down
  Must answer for your raising? I know her well:
  She had her breeding at my father's charge.
  A poor physician's daughter my wife! Disdain
  Rather corrupt me ever.

That is emphatically spoken indeed; and we can see how on the field of battle, where the moral issues were elementary, Bertram would have shone. But his resistance is a mere unguarded flare-up, and he soon collapses.

This moral cowardice joined to physical courage most characterizes Bertram and explains his actions, making him not only mean and repellent but pathetic and to be pitied. It is in the last two acts that Shakespeare develops and illustrates this defect of Bertram, just as he had done Helena's qualities in the earlier part of the play. Here he gives us, with brilliant insight into human nature, the processes by which Bertram quite gives way in the matters where he had most resisted. Part of that process takes place in IV. 3, the night-scene into which so much of the play's action is crowded, and part in the last scene of all. At the beginning of IV. 3 Bertram has achieved the utmost self-assertion of which he was capable. He has defied his mother (and public opinion generally) in refusing to acknowledge his wife, he has defied the French King in stealing away from Paris to the wars, he has defied conventional morality by succeeding, as he thinks, in seducing Diana. Further he has risked being proved wrong by allowing Parolles to be tested, and he has violated his own sense of family loyalty by surrendering his ancestral ring to Diana. The scene itself, though largely occupied with the comic business of Parolles's unmasking, mainly recounts the heavy series of blows to Bertram's confidence in the various acts of defiance he has committed. First there is his mother's letter: 'there is something in't that stings his nature; for on his reading it he changed almost into another man'. And it is not for nothing that these words come just before the pious words, quoted above, about the depravity of natural man. Bertram, though depraved, has still got a sensitive conscience. Next we hear of the French King's high displeasure. Then we hear of Helena's supposed death through grief ('the tenderness of her nature became as a prey to her grief in fine, made a groan of her last breath and now she sings in heaven'); and in view of the effect the Countess's letter had on Bertram we are expected to assume some remorse for this death. But this death has another consequence: his seduction of Diana has become serious, for he could now marry her. It has been a heavy series of blows, but for the moment he keeps control of himself and bluffs it all out with a brutal callousness and a bravado which we know conceal an inner qualm:

I have tonight dispatched sixteen businesses, a month's length a-piece, by an abstract of success. I have congied with the duke, done my adieu with his nearest; buried a wife, mourned for her; writ to my lady mother I am returning; entertained my convoy: and between these main parcels of dispatch effected many nicer needs. The last was the greatest, but that I have not ended yet. . . . The business is not ended, as fearing to hear of it hereafter.

This last business was the supposed seduction of Diana; and his fear on that score is both the index of his habit of mind and the connecting link with the last scene of the play. There follows the unmasking of Parolles, which Bertram watches in sullen anger – not, like the others, with fun. As Parolles grows more explicit and imaginative in his lies, one of the French Lords says 'He hath outvillained villany so far, that the rarity redeems him'. To which Bertram replies angrily 'A pox on him, he's a cat still'. The events of the night leave Bertram thoroughly shaken.

Sir Arthur Quiller-Couch, in his introduction to the New Cambridge edition of the play, sought to mitigate the unpleasantness of Bertram's character, but could not extend the mitigation to his behaviour in the last scene. I do not think there is any discrepancy. Bertram's nerve had been thoroughly undermined by the events just related; he was frightened of Diana. When confronted with her, his nerve gives way still more and he resorts in panic to any lie that will serve his turn. This exhibition of human nature is ignoble and unpleasant to witness, but it is perfectly true to the facts. Then, when the whole truth is out and Helena reappears, Bertram gives in completely. His former pursuer is now his saviour from a conspiracy of people and events which has overwhelmed him. And when to Helena's lovely complaint that she is but the shadow of a wife, the name but not the thing, he replies 'Both, both, O, pardon!', there is not the least cause for doubting his sincerity. However true it may be that the Elizabethans would expect and accept such a revulsion of feeling, there is no need to invoke such expectations to justify a situation assumed to be incredible to a modern. Psychological truth and the conventions of the fairy-tale are here at one. And when Bertram goes on to say that he will love Helena 'dearly, ever dearly', we should believe him implicitly. Helena has got her man; and he needs her moral support with such pathetic obviousness that she never need fear his escape.

Notes on *All's Well That Ends Well*

Helpful criticism of this play is scarce. The relevant sections of Van Doren's and Alexander's books have helped me most. I have mentioned Sir Arthur Quiller-Couch's good and sympathetic account of Bertram, but on many points I disagree with him completely. For instance (p. xxv), he considered Parolles an accretion:

Apart from the business of the drum and his exposure as a poltroon, all Parolles does is to engage Helena early in chat which he intends to be bawdy.

Parolles, though a light-weight as a character, is Bertram's evil genius and essential to the balance of the play. E. E. Stoll has an interesting chapter (xiii) on *All's Well* and *Measure for Measure* in his *From Shakespeare to Joyce* (New York, 1944). I go a good way with him, but disagree too on many points.

MEASURE FOR MEASURE

MEASURE FOR MEASURE has been singularly apt to provoke its critics to excess; and in the most different manners. Earlier critics vented their excesses on two of the main characters, Isabella and the Duke. Later critics have, in reaction to the earlier, gone to two different extremes. Some, in righteous and justified defence of the play's heroine, have refused to see any fault in the play at all; others, rightly recognizing a strong religious tone, have sought to give the whole play an allegorical and religious explanation. This is not to say that the above critics have not written well of the play. Many of them have; but nearly all have yoked their truths to strong and palpable errors. If I now proceed to enumerate some of the errors, it does not mean that I fail to recognize and pay tribute to the truths.

I begin with an earlier type of criticism. To an age whose typical mistake in criticism was to judge the persons of Elizabethan plays by the standards of actual life it is very natural that the Duke should be offensive. He is an eavesdropper; he chose as his deputy a man whom he knew to have behaved shabbily to his betrothed lady; and he displayed the utmost cruelty in concealing from Isabella for longer than was strictly necessary the news that her brother still lived. Certainly, as a real person, he is a most unsympathetic character; and though we may feel wiser than the Victorians and find no difficulty in the Duke as an allegorical figure or as a convenient stage machine, we can understand Victorian resentment. With Isabella the case is different.

Here is a character who, in those parts of the play where she really counts, will stand up to the test of the most rigid realism; and yet how they hated her! – this hard, smug, self-righteous virgin, preferring her own precious chastity to the actual life of a far more sympathetic person, her brother, and then, having got the utmost kick out of her militant virginity, having it both ways by consenting to marry the Duke at the end of the play. This actual error of interpretation no longer requires refutation. There is a fine defence of Isabella in R. W. Chambers's British Academy Shakespeare Lecture for 1937, the *Jacobean Shakespeare and 'Measure for Measure'*, while trouble, not long before that date, over the royal succession had revealed latent in the British public at large superstitious feelings on the virtue of chastity that had their bearing on the way Shakespeare's audience would have taken Isabella's problem. Not that these happenings were necessary to point to the truth; for the definitive interpretation of Isabella's action was given by Walter Scott when he prefixed quotations from *Measure for Measure* to some of his culminating chapters in the *Heart of Midlothian*. Before the twentieth chapter, when Effie Deans in prison pleads with her sister Jeanie to save her life by swearing to something which she cannot know to be true, Scott set these lines:

> Sweet sister, let me live;
> What sin you do to save a brother's life,
> Nature dispenses with the deed so far,
> That it becomes a virtue.

Isabella and Jeanie Deans are, as characters, very different women; yet Scott knew that he was here competing with Shakespeare and that Jeanie's problem was Isabella's problem. Jeanie's regard for truth was, like Isabella's for chastity, a matter of fundamental principle, a condition of life's validity. And both regards were equally redeemed from hypocrisy through their holders being less reluctant to sacrifice their own lives than to contribute by their ineluctable inaction to the required sacrifice of the lives of their kin. Let anyone who doubts how Shakespeare meant the principal episodes in *Measure for Measure* (and none of these occurs after the first scene of Act Three) to be taken read or re-read these culminating episodes of the *Heart of Midlothian*, including Jeanie's resolution to go to London to obtain a royal pardon for her sister. Not only will he learn how to take the first half of *Measure for Measure* but he should note that in the play there is nothing to correspond to Jeanie Deans's journey to London in the novel.

So much generally for Isabella's nature and motives. Why was it that many readers mistook them? Partly, I think, because of an unfortunate habit of treating Shakespeare's heroines as a repertory of ideal brides, quite detached, poor things, from their native dramatic settings. If *you* were a young man, free to choose a bride, would it be Miranda or Beatrice? Wasn't Beatrice something of a risk? And wouldn't you really be safer with Portia? Yes, perhaps, if your tastes were high-brow enough. And so on, and so on. You will find that a proportion of writing on Shakespeare's heroines was conducted on those lines. Now Isabella comes off very ill on such a criterion. The husbands of such female saints or martyrs as were married have, as far as I know, never been the object of much envy; the role of martyr-consort is a hard one. And such would have been that of Isabella's husband. And so the day-dreaming bride-pickers very naturally found her distasteful and turned and rent her. And yet, in defending her, we must not forget that in the play Isabella marries and in so doing makes herself the more open to irrelevant comparisons. Her enemies have at least that excuse for their attacks; and her friends, like R. W. Chambers, however well justified in defending her behaviour towards her brother, have erred in justifying the sum total of her conduct.

This brings me to the other type of error, which is roughly that of seeing nothing wrong with the play. There are several ways of establishing it. One (and I here think mainly of R. W. Chambers) is to begin by making hay of the mythical sorrows of Shakespeare and of the mythical hypocrisy of Isabella and to go on to prove that the high ethical standards set in the first half are maintained and carried through in the second. And the proof can be fascinating. Nothing could be more ingenious and plausible than Chambers's notion of Shakespeare's keeping Isabella ignorant of her brother's survival and filled with justified fury at Angelo's having done him to death, in order that her powers of forgiveness might be tested to the uttermost when she brings herself to join Mariana in pleading for Angelo's life. And how much more creditable to Shakespeare and pleasanter to most of us, to whom his credit is very dear, if he did in fact keep Isabella in the dark for so high and moral a motive and not merely to pander to that appetite for ingenious plot-complications and improbable and strained moments of suspense which was one of the regrettable qualities of an Elizabethan audience. Nothing, too, could help to colour the last part of the play more happily than a truly heartfelt and impressive repentance on the part of Angelo. And, relying on the undoubted truth that Angelo does profess himself very repentant, Chambers does duly find Angelo's repentance very impressive. The other way to find the play faultless is to cut out all the Bradleian character-stuff from the start and to go straight to ideas or allegory or symbols. There is much thought and much orthodox piety in *Measure for Measure*, and during the time when Shakespeare was writing the Problem Plays he had the Morality form rather prominently in his mind. That in some sort the relation of justice and mercy is treated, that Angelo may stand at one time for the letter of the law or for the old law before Christian liberty and at another for a Morality figure of False Seeming, that the Duke contains hints of heavenly Grace and that he embodies a higher justice than mere legality, that Isabella is Mercy as well as Chastity – all these matters may very likely be concluded from the text and they may help us to understand the play. But they are conclusions which are ineffective in just the same way in which Chambers's theories on Isabella's ignorance and Angelo's repentance are ineffective: they have little to do with the total play, however justifiable they may appear by these and those words or passages in abstraction. Now the doctrinal or allegorical significance of *Measure for Measure* culminates in the last long scene. And this scene does not succeed whether witnessed or read. Its main effect is that of labour. Shakespeare took trouble; he complicated enormously; he brought a vast amount of dramatic matter together. The actors know it is a big scene and they try to make it go. Perhaps their efforts just succeed; but then the success will be a tribute more to their efforts than to the scene itself. In the strain the supposed subtle reason for Isabella's ignorance of Claudio's survival goes unnoticed, while Angelo's repentance is a perfunctory affair amidst all the other crowded doings. Similarly, fresh from reading or seeing the play, how little aware we are of any allegorical motive. Even if the Duke stands for Providence, he does not begin to interpose till after the first and incomparably the better half of the play. Claudio and Juliet may have been designed by their author to represent unregenerate mankind; yet Claudio at his first appearance is in a highly chastened and penitent frame of mind, well on the road to salvation: as when he says,

> The words of heaven: on whom it will, it will;
> On whom it will not, so. Yet still 'tis just.

Claudio is paraphrasing scripture, namely St Paul's words in Romans ix: 'Therefore hath he mercy on whom he will have mercy, and whom he will he hardeneth'. But though he may class himself among the hardened sinners on account of his misdeed, there is no hardness left in him now. And quite apart from whether Claudio can, from his words, represent the unregenerate *homo* of the Moralities, he does in fact show himself to us first and foremost as a most unfortunate young man, deeply to be pitied.

The simple and ineluctable fact is that the tone in the first half of the play is frankly, acutely human and quite hostile to the tone of allegory or symbol. And, however much the tone changes in the second half, nothing in the world can make an allegorical interpretation poetically valid throughout.

Recent critics, in their anxiety to correct old errors, have in fact gone too far in the other direction and ignored one of the prime facts from which those old errors had their origin: namely that the play is not of a piece but changes its nature half-way through. It was partly through their correct perception of something being wrong that some earlier critics felt justified in making the Isabella of the first half of the play the scapegoat of the play's imperfections.

The above inconsistency has long been noted, but since of late it has been so strongly denied, I had better assert it once more, and if possible not quite in the old terms. Briefly, the inconsistency is the most serious and complete possible, being one of literary style. Up to III. 1. 151, when the Duke enters to interrupt the passionate conversation between Claudio and Isabella on the conflicting claims of his life and her chastity, the play is predominantly poetical, the poetry being, it is true, set off by passages of animated prose. And the poetry is of that kind of which Shakespeare is the great master, the kind that seems extremely close to the business of living, to the problem of how to function as a human being. One character after another is pictured in a difficult, a critical, position, and yet one which all of us can imagine ourselves to share; and the poetry answers magnificently to this penetrating sense of human intimacy. Up to the above point the Duke, far from being guide and controller, has been a mere conventional piece of dramatic convenience for creating the setting for the human conflicts. Beyond that he is just an onlooker. And, as pointed out above, any symbolic potentialities the characters may possess are obscured by the tumult of passions their minds present to us. From the Duke's entry at III. 1. 151 to the end of the play there is little poetry of any kind and scarcely any of the kind described above. There is a passage of beautiful verse spoken by the Provost, Claudio, and the Duke in the prison, IV. 2. 66 ff. Take these lines from it:

> PROVOST: It is a bitter deputy.
> DUKE: Not so, not so: his life is parallel'd
>   Even with the stroke and line of his great justice.
>   He doth with holy abstinence subdue
>   That in himself which he spurs on his power
>   To qualify in others. Were he meal'd with that
>   Which he corrects, then were he tyrannous;
>   But this being so, he's just.

In their way these lines cannot be bettered but they do not touch the great things in the early part of the play; their accent is altogether more subdued. Again, the episode of Mariana and Isabella pleading to the Duke for Angelo's life, in the last scene of all, does rise somewhat as poetry. But this exceptional passage counts for little in the prevailing tone of lowered poetical tension. Where in the first half the most intense writing was poetical, in the second half it is comic or at least prosaic. While the elaborate last scene, as I have already pointed out, for all its poetical pretensions is either a dramatic failure or at best a Pyrrhic victory, it is the comedy of Lucio and the Duke, of Pompey learning the mystery of the executioner from Abhorson, of Barnardine (for Shakespeare somehow contrives to keep his gruesomeness this side the comic) that makes the second half of the play possible to present on the stage with any success at all. And the vehicle of this comedy is prose, which, excellent though it is, cannot be held consistent with the high poetry of the first half. Another evident sign of tension relaxed in the second half of the play is the increased use of rhyme. Not that it occurs in such long stretches as in *All's Well*; but there are many short passages, like this soliloquy of the Duke after hearing Lucio's scandalous remarks on his character in III. 2:

> No might nor greatness in mortality
> Can censure 'scape; back-wounding calumny
> The whitest virtue strikes. What king so strong
> Can tie the gall up in the sland'rous tongue?

or the couplet containing the title of the play:

> Haste still pays haste, and leisure answers leisure;
> Like doth quit like, and Measure still for Measure.

Here an antique quaintness excuses the lack of poetic intensity. Most characteristic of this quality in the last half of the play are the Duke's octosyllabic couplets at the end of III. 2:

> He who the sword of heaven will bear
> Should be as holy as severe:
> Pattern in himself to know,
> Grace to stand, and virtue go;
> More nor less to others paying
> Than by self-offences weighing –

and the rest. Far from being spurious, the Duke's couplets in their antique stiffness and formality agree with the whole trend of the play's second half in relaxing the poetical tension and preparing for a more abstract form of drama.

A similar inconsistency extends to some of the characters. From being a minor character in the first half, with no influence on the way human motives are presented, the Duke becomes the dominant character in the second half and the one through whose mind human motives are judged. In the first half of the play we are in the very thick of action, where different human beings have their own special and different problems and are concerned with how to settle them. Mistress Overdone's problem of what's to be done now all the houses of resort in the suburbs are to be pulled down stands on its own feet quite separate from Claudio's problem of what's to be done now he has been arrested. We are in fact too close to them both to be able to distance them into a single perspective or a common unifying colour. Reality is too urgent to allow of reflection. In the second half the Duke is in charge. He has his plans, and, knowing they will come to fruition, we can watch their workings. Reflection has encroached on reality. W. W. Lawrence wrote a fine chapter on *Measure for Measure*, in which he points to the Duke's multifarious functions. The Duke's part derives both from the old folk-motive of the sovereign in disguise mixing with his people and from the conventional stage-character of the plot-promoting priest. He combines the functions of church and state. In his disguise he 'represents the wisdom and adroitness of the Church in directing courses of action and advising stratagems so that good may come out of evil'. He is also the supreme ruler of Vienna who at the end 'straightens out the tangles of the action and dispenses justice to all'. He is also a stage figure, highly important for manipulating the action and contrasted strikingly with the realistic characters. Admitting most truly that 'Shakespeare's art oscillates between extreme psychological subtlety and an equally extreme disregard of psychological truth, in the acceptance of stock narrative conventions', Lawrence may imply that the Duke does succeed in uniting these extremes. If so, I can only disagree, because Lawrence's description of the Duke applies only faintly to the first half of the play.

Nowhere does the change in the Duke's position show so strikingly as in Isabella. There is no more independent character in Shakespeare than the Isabella of the first half of the play: and independent in two senses. The essence of her disposition is decision and the acute sense of her own independent and inviolate personality; while her own particular problem of how to act is presented with all that differentiation which I attributed to the problems of Claudio and Mistress Overdone. At the beginning of the third act, when she has learnt Angelo's full villainy, her nature is working at the very height of its accustomed freedom. She enters almost choked with bitter fury at Angelo, in the mood for martyrdom and feeling that Claudio's mere life is a trifle before the mighty issues of right and wrong. Her scorn of Claudio's weakness is dramatically definitive and perfect. To his pathetic pleas, 'Sweet sister, let me live' etc., the lines Scott prefixed to the twentieth chapter of the *Heart of Midlothian*, comes, as it must, her own, spontaneous retort from the depth of her being,

> O you beast,
> O faithless coward, O dishonest wretch!
> Wilt thou be made a man out of my vice?
> Is't not a kind of incest to take life
> From thine own sister's shame? What should I think?
> Heaven shield my mother play'd my father fair,
> For such a warped slip of wilderness
> Ne'er issued from his blood. Take my defiance,
> Die, perish! Might but my bending down
> Reprieve thee from thy fate, it should proceed.
> I'll pray a thousand prayers for thy death,
> No word to save thee.

That is the true Isabella, and whether or not we like that kind of woman is beside the point. But immediately after her speech, at line 152, the Duke takes charge and she proceeds to exchange her native ferocity for the hushed and submissive tones of a well-trained confidential secretary. To the Duke's inquiry of how she will content Angelo and save her brother she replies in coolly rhetorical prose:

I am now going to resolve him: I had rather my brother die by the law than my son should be unlawfully born. But, O, how much is the good duke deceived in Angelo! If ever he return and I can speak to him, I will open my lips in vain or discover his government.

But such coolness is warm compared with her tame acquiescence in the Duke's plan for her to pretend to yield to Angelo and then to substitute Mariana:

The image of it gives me content already, and I trust it will grow to a most prosperous perfection.

To argue, as has been argued, that the plan, by Elizabethan standards, was very honourable and sensible and that of course Isabella would have accepted it gladly is to substitute the criterion of ordinary practical common sense for that of the drama. You could just as well seek to compromise the fictional validity of Jeanie Deans's journey to London by proving that the initial practical difficulties of such a journey at such a date rendered the undertaking highly improbable. In Scott's novel Jeanie Deans does travel to London, and, though Scott had better have shorn her journey of many of its improbable and romantic complications, it is a consistent Jeanie Deans who takes the journey, and her action in taking the journey and in pleading with the Queen is significant. Isabella, on the contrary, has been bereft of significant action, she has nothing to do corresponding to Jeanie's journey, and she has turned into a mere tool of the Duke. In the last scene she does indeed bear some part in the action; but her freedom of utterance is so hampered by misunderstanding and mystification that she never speaks with her full voice: she is not, dramatically, the same Isabella. That the Duke is in his way impressive, that he creates a certain moral atmosphere, serious and yet tolerant, in the second half of the play need not be denied; yet that atmosphere can ill bear comparison with that of the early part of the play. To this fact Lucio is the chief witness. He is now the livest figure and the one who does most to keep the play from quite falling apart, and he almost eludes the Duke's control. He is as it were a minor Saturnian deity who has somehow survived into the iron age of Jupiter; and a constant reminder that the Saturnian age was the better of the two.

The fact of the play's inconsistency, then, seems to me undoubted: the reason for it must be conjectural, yet conjectural within not excessive bounds of probability. I believe it may be found through considering Shakespeare's originals.

The plot of *Measure for Measure* goes back to one or both versions of a similar story by George Whetstone. The earlier is a play in two parts called *Promos and Cassandra* and published in 1578, the later a short narrative called the *Rare History of Promos and Cassandra* and included in his story-collection called the *Heptameron of Civil Discourses*, 1582. Behind both versions is a story of Cinthio. I think Shakespeare was indebted to both versions. He certainly must have known the play, for this contains, as the narrative does not, scenes of low life that correspond to similar scenes in *Measure for Measure*. There is also the incident (*Promos and Cassandra*, Part 2, v. 5) when Polina (=Juliet), though wronged by Promos (=Angelo) through the death of her plighted lover, Andrugio (=Claudio), joins Cassandra (=Isabella, but in this version of the story married ultimately to Promos) in praying God to relieve Promos. It is not found in the narrative and it seems to be behind the incident in *Measure for Measure* of Isabella joining Mariana to plead for Angelo although he has done her brother Claudio to death. But the way Shakespeare deals with the theme of the principles of justice is nearer the narrative. There is a lot about justice in Whetstone's play, including disquisitions on the true meaning of what Shakespeare called measure for measure. But there is more about the wickedness of bribery in the government and the need for the magistrate to be a pattern of virtue. It is in the narrative that the theme of what true justice is predominates. That Shakespeare was drawn to that theme, and possibly in the first stages of roughing out his plot, may be conjectured.

But there were things in Whetstone's play that kindled his imagination more warmly than the theory of justice, whether derived from narrative or drama. Whetstone's best scene (and even so it is a very poor affair) is Part 1, III. 4 where Cassandra debates with her brother Andrugio and with herself whether she will let him die or whether she will yield her honour to Promos. Like Isabella she would gladly die in place of her brother and she thinks death in itself a lesser evil than loss of honour. But Andrugio points out that Promos might after all end by marrying her and then all might be well. And Cassandra is so impressed by this argument that she decides to save her brother. However feeble the scene, it does present to the reader or the re-caster certain simple and basic human passions and conflicts: Promos's dilemma between justice and lust; Andrugio's instinct to save his life at almost any cost; Cassandra's dilemma between the desires to save her brother's life and to save her honour. The human interest and the dramatic possibilities of these passions and conflicts kindled Shakespeare's imagination and he proceeded in the first half of *Measure for Measure* to give his version of them.

But in so doing he altered Whetstone in one very important matter: he made his heroine resist the appeal of her brother to save his life. In accordance with this change he turns his heroine into a much more decided and uncompromising person. In Whetstone the chief dramatic interest is the heroine's divided mind, her struggle with herself: Shakespeare's heroine has a whole mind and has no struggle with herself: all her struggles are outside, with her brother and her would-be seducer. It looks as if Shakespeare had been carried away by his conception of Isabella without realizing the dramatic difficulties it involved. Whetstone's Cassandra, however inferior in execution to Shakespeare's Isabella, was through her very weakness a more flexible dramatic character. Her mind, divided once, can be divided again and provide interesting dramatic situations. After Promos has enjoyed her, he decides nevertheless to have Andrugio killed, because to spare him would be to show partiality in the eyes of the world. Actually Andrugio is spared and set free by his jailers, but neither Promos nor Cassandra knows this. Hearing of Andrugio's supposed death, Cassandra would like to take her own life. But, then, she reflects, Andrugio will lack an avenger; and her mind is divided between the desires for death and for revenge. The first part of the play ends with Cassandra's resolve to take her life only after having appealed to the King for vengeance. Yet a third struggle occurs when the King, hearing of Promos's crimes, has him married to Cassandra, and then orders his death. As Andrugio predicted, marriage puts everything right between Promos and Cassandra; and Cassandra is now divided between loyalty to a dead brother and loyalty to a new, living, husband. The second loyalty prevails. Little as Whetstone made of the play's dramatic possibilities, he did at least allow those possibilities to permeate the whole story consistently. Shakespeare by altering the plot and by re-creating his heroine, however superb the immediate result, could only ruin the play as a whole. Not having been violated, Isabella has no call to meditate suicide. Not having become Angelo's wife, she has no reason to recommend him to mercy as well as to justice. Her one possible line of action was to appeal outright to the Duke; and that would be to sabotage most of the substance of the last half of the play. With significant action denied to Isabella, Shakespeare must have seen that to carry the play through in the spirit in which he began it was impossible; and after III. 1. 151 he threw in his hand.

Whether in the second half Shakespeare reverted to an original plan from which he had played truant, or whether he began to improvise when he found himself stuck, we shall never know. But conjecture may be easier when we recognize the large differences in the material from which he derived the two portions of his play. That we can do so is largely due to W. W. Lawrence. Lawrence distinguishes two kinds of material in *Measure for Measure*. The central episode of a sister having to decide whether to save her brother's life at the expense of her honour may go back to a historical incident and anyhow is related to real life and not to folk-lore. Similarly the setting in the low life of a city, not found before Whetstone, is realistic and not traditional or magical. But Shakespeare grafted onto the realistic material of Whetstone two themes that belong to the world of the fairy-tale: first, the disguised king mingling with and observing his own people, and second the secret substitution of the real bride in the husband's bed. At first sight the case seems to be much that of *All's*

Well. There we have a highly realistic setting and array of characters, to which are attached the folk-themes of the person who by healing a king obtains a boon, of the setting of certain seemingly impossible tasks, and of the substitute bride. But actually the cases are very different and suggest that the plays were differently put together. In *All's Well* realism and folk-lore are blended from beginning to end; in *Measure for Measure* realism admits no folk-lore for half of the play, while all the folk-lore occurs in the second half. The same is true of allegory. The notions of Helena standing in some way for an emissary of heaven and of Bertram as a Morality figure drawn on one side by his mother and bride to good and on the other by Parolles to evil, faint in themselves, are yet spread throughout the play. Corresponding notions of the Duke as Heavenly Justice, or Isabella as Mercy, and so forth, though in themselves more evident and stronger than their parallels in *All's Well*, are quite absent from the first part of the play and appear quite suddenly in the second. It looks therefore as if *All's Well*, however deficient in execution, was conceived and executed consistently and with no change of mind, but as if the two types of material from which *Measure for Measure* was drawn betoken two different types of execution, and an abrupt change from one to the other. Exactly what happened in Shakespeare's mind we shall never know. He may or may not have meant initially to write a play on the great themes of justice, mercy, and forgiveness. If he did, he seems to have changed his mind and sought above all to give his own version of the human potentialities of Whetstone's theme. Self-defeated half-way, through the turn he gave that theme, he may have reverted to his original, more abstract intentions, to help him out. More likely, to my thinking, he sought help from the methods and the incidents of the play, written shortly before and still in temper akin to his present self, *All's Well that Ends Well*.

It is, incidentally, because the folk-material is so differently spaced and blended in the two plays that the theme of the substitute bride is quite seemly in *All's Well* and is somehow rather shocking in *Measure for Measure*. In *All's Well* we have been habituated to the improbable, the conventional, and the antique: in *Measure for Measure* the change to these from the more lifelike human passions is too violent; and it is here a case not of a modern prudery unaware of Elizabethan preconceptions but of an artistic breach of internal harmony.

But I am loth to end on matters mainly conjectural, and I will revert to the first half of *Measure for Measure* and pay my tribute to a quality in it that has not quite had its due. Full justice can never be done to what Shakespeare really achieved here, on account of the imperfections of our only text, that of the First Folio. For instance, scene II. 4, when Angelo tempts Isabella to buy Claudio's life by her virtue, is terribly obscure in places and simply cannot be read with unimpeded pleasure. But in spite of textual impediments it has been recognized that the prevailing style matches that of *Hamlet* and possibly of *Othello*. This comment of Claudio on Angelo and his new official zeal has surely the accent of *Hamlet*:

> And the new deputy now for the Duke –
> Whether it be the fault and glimpse of newness,
> Or whether that the body public be
> A horse whereon the governor doth ride,
> Who, newly in the seat, that it may know
> He can command, lets it straight feel the spur;
> Whether the tyranny be in his place
> Or in his eminence that fills it up,
> I stagger in – but this new governor
> Awakes me all the enrolled penalties
> Which have like unscour'd armour hung by the wall
> So long that nineteen zodiacs have gone round
> And none of them been worn; and, for a name,
> Now puts the drowsy and neglected act
> Freshly on me.
>
> (i. 2. 161–75)

The power of the verse in the early part of *Measure for Measure* has indeed been allowed. Less notice has been taken of the extreme subtlety of characterization. I will illustrate this from scene II. 2, where Isabella, seconded by Lucio, first pleads with Angelo for her brother's life. It is a scene whose power is obvious and has been generally admitted. Close reading is necessary to bring out the accompanying subtlety with which all the movements of Isabella's mind are presented. At first Shakespeare risks failure by asserting psychological truth almost at the expense of dramatic probability. Isabella begins her attack on Angelo with a crudity and a lack of strategy which on a first impact are staggering:

> There is a vice that most I do abhor
> And most desire should meet the blow of justice;
> For which I would not plead but that I must;
> For which I must not plead but that I am
> At war 'twixt will and will not.

Yet this crudity is absolutely natural. Claudio's arrest could not, from Isabella's point of view, have been timed worse. Young, ardent, neophytic, she has bent all her strength to embrace an other-worldly ideal. And in the very act of embracement she is called on to plead in mitigation of that which is most abhorrent to her. Her crude self-explanation is psychologically inevitable. And what is so brilliant in the rest of the scene is the way in which she gradually discards the drawing-in of herself into cloistral concentration and reaches out again to a worldly observation she has newly renounced. And that observation includes a bitter anger that this mere man, this Angelo, this precisian, should be able to decide her brother's fate.

At first she is helpless and is for giving over at the first rebuff:

> O just but severe law!
> I had a brother then. Heaven keep your honour!

But Lucio intervenes and urges her to a fresh attack. The best she can do now is to recall and utter some current commonplaces about mercy and about the judge being no better than the accused. But her accent is, surely, still formal and cool:

> Well, believe this,
> No ceremony that to great ones 'longs,
> Not the king's crown, nor the deputed sword,
> The marshal's truncheon, nor the judge's robe,
> Become them with one half so good a grace
> As mercy does.

But something, whether an unconscious clash of wills or a secret sense of Angelo's being stirred by her own self, prompts Isabella to be personal and she goes on:

> If he had been as you and you as he
> You would have slipt like him; but he like you
> Would not have been so stern.

And when Angelo tells her to be gone, at once her personal opposition stiffens, and, no longer the awesome wielder of the law and God's deputy, he becomes in her eyes mere man and as deeply in need of God's mercy as any sinner. Her renewed plea for mercy is now impassioned, and when he tells her that Claudio must die tomorrow he arouses the whole stretch of her mind. Her concern for Claudio is cruelly sharpened and prompts her to the kind of humour that lies next to the tragic:

> He's not prepared for death. Even for our kitchens
> We kill the fowl of season. Shall we serve heaven
> With less respect than we do minister
> To our gross selves?

Angelo still resists but feels called on to defend his action at greater length. His cold pompousness infuriates her and calls forth her culminating and classic denunciation of human pride. But first by her bitter emphasis on the personal pronouns she makes it plain that her attack on pride is far from being on an abstract and impersonal sin:

> So *you* must be the first that gives this sentence,
> And *he*, that suffers.

And we do Shakespeare's art less than justice if, absorbed in the detachable splendour of the lines that follow, we forget the personal application.

> O, it is excellent
> To have a giant's strength; but it is tyrannous
> To use it like a giant. Could great men thunder
> As Jove himself does, Jove would ne'er be quiet;
> For every pelting, petty officer
> Would use his heaven for thunder, nothing but thunder.
> Merciful heaven,
> Thou rather with thy sharp and sulphurous bolt
> Splits the unwedgeable and gnarled oak
> Than the soft myrtle. But man, proud man,
> Drest in a little brief authority,
> Most ignorant of what he's most assur'd,
> His glassy essence, like an angry ape
> Plays such fantastic tricks before high heaven
> As make the angels weep; who, with our spleens
> Would all themselves laugh mortal.

Such eloquence cannot lack effect. Lucio (and we may assume Isabella too) sees that some change is taking place in Angelo. There is one kind of irony in Isabella's and a very different kind in Lucio's, who must have prided himself on his connoisseurship of the tokens of lust, being quite deceived as to the nature of that change. Isabella, now confident of victory, speaks less vehemently, and Lucio, anxious lest too much of the same thing may spoil the victory, signals for them to go at once, when Angelo says he will see Isabella again tomorrow.

The whole scene, and especially Isabella's speech on pride, illustrates the truth that in the drama the most powerful general effect comes by way of absorption into the immediate dramatic business, just as writers in general are most likely to speak to all ages when most sensitive to the spiritual climate of their own. Here, at any rate, problem play or no problem play, Shakespeare is at the height of his strength.

Notes on *Measure for Measure*

There is a useful account of recent criticism of the play in Roy W. Battenhouse's '*Measure for Measure*' *and Christian Doctrine* in *Publications of the Modern Language Association of America*, 1946, pp. 1029–59. But Battenhouse's theory that the play is an allegory of the Atonement I find over-ingenious and unconvincing. For the Morality theme in *Measure for Measure* see Muriel C. Bradbrook in *Review of English Studies*, 1941, pp. 385 ff.

EPILOGUE

IN my introduction I pointed to certain resemblances within the Problem Plays. It remains to ask in what ways these plays look forward or take their place in Shakespeare's general progress as a dramatist.

I made out *Hamlet* to be a tragedy only in a limited sense. Its success in that sense may have prompted Shakespeare to attempt something further: a less restricted form of tragedy. I have not noticed in *Troilus and Cressida* anything that looks forward. It has analogies with contemporary Elizabethan drama, and in a certain point of style it looks back to *Henry V*. But it is not seminal. The truly seminal plays are *All's Well* and *Measure for Measure*: and it remains to say how these lead on to a further Shakespearean efflorescence.

Those who think these plays essentially bitter and satirical will have no use for what follows, which rests on the belief that, however much incidental gloom or bitterness may be there, the themes of mercy and forgiveness are sincerely and not ironically presented. Bertram is made out a very unpleasant young man, but we are not meant to take his forgiveness by the French King and by his wife to be a cynical comment on how in this world the wicked prosper. We must accept Isabella quite simply for what she is and refuse to consider her as a vicious comment on how inhumanly a self-centred and pious prude can behave. Through Angelo Shakespeare certainly does convey the dreadful limitation and inequity of mere legality. But the portrait is not primarily satirical and takes its place in a context of sincere tolerance and forgiveness. In both plays Shakespeare is more positive than negative, more *for* certain things than *against* certain other things. The themes therefore of mercy and forgiveness are genuine as well as prominent, and they unite *All's Well* and *Measure for Measure* with *Cymbeline*, the *Winter's Tale*, and the *Tempest*. But the ethically genuine and the dramatically successful are not the same. No one of course claims high success for *All's Well*, yet *Measure for Measure* has been put, as a drama of forgiveness, on a level with the *Winter's Tale*. This, I believe, is to confuse the above two qualities and to fail really to read *Measure for Measure*. On the other hand it is plain that long before Shakespeare wrote his last plays he wanted to treat the theme of forgiveness; and his early artistic failures can hardly not be related to his later successes. It remains to trace this relation.

In both the earlier plays there is one main object of forgiveness, Bertram in one and Angelo in the other. Secondary to Bertram is Parolles, and to Angelo a number of people. The technique of both plays is to accumulate through their course matters standing in need of forgiveness; and to postpone the time of reckoning to a long and elaborate last scene. Such scenes, where large numbers of characters are gathered together, where sections of these characters are ignorant of facts known to other sections while the audience knows everything, must have tickled the Elizabethan taste. They have not stood the test of time and emerge as melodramatic rather than dramatic, giving the serious the taint of frivolity. Treated thus, the theme of forgiveness could never succeed. Apart from this staking so much on a grand finale, there is the problem, recurrent in Shakespeare, of how to avoid bathos between a climax occurring about the middle of the play and the renewed elevation of the ending. In both plays Shakespeare fills in with comic business between characters already introduced. In *All's Well*, where the poetical level has never been high, this succeeds perfectly well within the limits of the play's possible success; in *Measure for Measure*, however good in itself, it cannot counterpoise the immensely powerful poetical effect achieved in the first half of the play.

Shakespeare's next play on the theme of forgiveness is *Cymbeline*, and it is closely allied to the earlier pair by repeating and even exaggerating the technique of the grand finale. Another resemblance is the way it mingles the material of real life and of folk-lore. But there are new elements derived from a related play but one in which the theme of forgiveness is not very prominent, *Pericles*. These elements are the finding of something lost. Cymbeline's two sons were lost in infancy and they appear later in the play leading a kind of existence new to anything hitherto revealed. The grand finale fails just as surely as in *All's Well* and *Measure for Measure*, though there is less mystification. But the scenes in Wales where Cymbeline's two sons figure do help to fill the awkward gap between the middle climax and the finale. The innovation is, technically, quite effective. But the play contains too much matter, and though it can pass, through the excellence of some of its verse, the splendour of some of the separate scenes, and a kind of pantomimic variety that helps it along when staged, it fails to make the theme of forgiveness significant.

At last, in the *Winter's Tale*, things come right. First, Shakespeare dropped the disastrous practice of the grand finale. He settled much of the necessary plotting and explanation through prose narrative and left only the minimum of recognition to be accomplished in the final scene of Hermione's statue. Here at last the theme of forgiveness has a worthy setting. Then he followed and improved on his success in *Cymbeline* in introducing new elements in that part of the play where bathos is most likely. If Guiderius and Arviragus in Wales help *Cymbeline* along, the lovely pastoral in Bohemia, the loves of Florizel and Perdita, and the splendour of Perdita herself, not only triumph technically in filling in a dangerous gap, but create that new life without which the mere forgiveness of old crimes is apt to be hollow. True forgiveness is not the cancellation of old debts, but the reduction to health of a life process that has been impeded and can now proceed once more.

But this is not the place to praise the *Winter's Tale*. Rather I must point out how much it has in common with *Measure for Measure*. First, it falls definitely into two halves, the division marked by a long lapse of time and a chorus. Secondly, there is an abrupt contrast between the tones of the two halves. The first half deals with violent human passions: jealousy, cruelty, persecution, and grief. The tone of the second, though intense and powerful in its way, is predominantly idyllic. Only in *Measure for Measure* of Shakespeare's other plays is there so sharp a cleavage in the middle and so sharp a change of tone from one section to the other. There is also the common theme of the supposed victim of the tyrant's cruelty being secretly kept alive. I believe Shakespeare had *Measure for Measure* in mind when he wrote the *Winter's Tale*; and I suspect that he was resolved to redeem that splendid failure.

It is natural that one play of Shakespeare should contain elements that are absorbed into another. Artists answer differently to the flux that life presents. We cannot suppose that the Athenians of the fifth century were less aware of that flux than the Elizabethans, yet their artists delighted in giving their art the greatest apparent fixity, in, as it were, crystallizing all possible elements of the flux into great static creations. Such must have been the nature of Phidias's Zeus at Olympia and his Virgin Athena at Athens. Shakespeare prefers a method closer to life's actual workings. He can indeed be monumental in certain scenes, but he is most himself when boundaries are not too glaring, when one part slides into another, when through a series of plays a notion is born, flowers, and is fulfilled. The three plays I have mainly dealt with are not any of them supreme in Shakespeare's canon but they are true to his typical kaleidoscopic genius. Of that canon they are a deeply interesting and a worthy part.

APPENDICES

Hamlet's Defiance of Augury (v. 2. 203–35)

The interpretation of this passage is crucial to the way the play as a whole is taken. I will discuss it here in more detail than would fit the text itself. Osric has just gone out, bearing with him to the King Hamlet's acceptance of the fencing-match. After a few words between Hamlet and Horatio a Lord enters and asks Hamlet if he is still agreeable to beginning the match at once. Hamlet answers,

I am constant to my purposes; they follow the King's pleasure; if his fitness speaks, mine is ready; now or whensoever, provided I be so able as now.

The Lord then says that the King and Queen will arrive shortly, and, adding that the Queen wishes Hamlet to be courteous to Laertes, goes out. Horatio and Hamlet then speak as follows:

HORATIO: You will lose this wager, my lord.
HAMLET: I do not think so. Since he went into France, I have been in continual practice; I shall win at the odds. But thou wouldst not think how ill all's here about my heart; but it is no matter.
HORATIO: Nay, good my lord –
HAMLET: It is but foolery; but it is such a kind of gain-giving as would perhaps trouble a woman.
HORATIO: If your mind dislike anything, obey it; I will forestall their repair hither and say you are not fit.

HAMLET: Not a whit, we defy augury; there's a special providence in the fall of a sparrow. If it be now, 'tis not to come; if it be not to come, it will be now; if it be not now, yet it will come; the readiness is all: since no man has aught of what he leaves, what is't to leave betimes? Let be.

If only one knew just what this passage implies, what a help in understanding the rest of *Hamlet*. But it is fatally easy to advance plausible and incompatible interpretations. I will put forward two, roughly to suit the two opposed notions of change or lack of change in Hamlet's mind.

1. Hamlet's answer to the Lord bears two meanings. As well as saying that Hamlet is still ready to fence at short notice, it means as follows: *I am constant to my purposes,* that is to kill Claudius; *they follow the King's pleasure,* my purposes seek out the occasion of 'the incestuous pleasure of his bed' or of some other pleasure 'that has no relish of salvation in't'; *if his fitness speaks, mine is ready,* if I find him in a case where death will be followed by the deepest damnation, I am ready to act; *now or whensoever, provided I be so able as now,* now or at any time, provided my present new mood of resolution holds. Hamlet, therefore, has thrown off his irresolution, he has made up his mind, and he proceeds to kill Claudius as the opportunity offers. Not only is he resolved to do his duty, but in his conversation with Horatio he shows that he had ceased to brood on the after-life and has put his trust in God. He will face death whenever it comes. Hamlet is thus doubly regenerate.

2. It is possible to take the passage at a much lower pitch of seriousness. Hamlet's reply to the Lord will bear no more than its surface meaning that he sticks to his willingness to fence, and that he will play the match at any time, provided he is in as good practice as he now is. His conversation with Horatio is not to be pressed too hard. He *does* feel a premonition, which serves a useful dramatic purpose in pointing forward to the end of the play. When he makes light of the premonition he does so rather in the

easy fatalistic mood of the soldier who repeats the stock phrase of every bullet's having its billet. The lightness of the final 'let be' is a true pointer to the spirit of the passage.

From the run of the prose I have no doubt myself that the second interpretation is correct and that the implications set forth in the first interpretation are fortuitous and not intentional. A. C. Bradley (*Shakespearean Tragedy*, pp. 144–6), though thinking Hamlet in some ways changed on his return to Denmark, thinks him unchanged in the main matter of his melancholy. He feels himself more than before in the hand of God, but the passages showing this do not show 'any material change in his general condition, or the formation of any effective resolution to fulfil his appointed duty'. He falls indeed into a kind of fatalism. I think Bradley right.

I suspect that 'the interim is mine', the crucial phrase in the verse preceding the prose from which the extract discussed above was taken, is ironic; for soon after the words he falls into the trap of the duel. The interim is, in fact, not his at all.

APPENDIX B

Why did Hamlet spare Claudius at his prayers?

In assessing Hamlet's motives for sparing Claudius at his prayers recent opinion has been over-suspicious of the psychological interpreters, who detect the presence of unacknowledged motives, and over-credulous of the 'tough' interpreters, who can take at its face value Hamlet's resolve to inflict nothing but the deepest damnation. However wrong the nineteenth century may have been in making the play only a psychological study, it is no better trying to rationalize it and reduce its motives to those of expediency and common sense. The world of *Hamlet* is one in which unexpressed motives are likely to count. There is no need to decide whether Hamlet would have killed Claudius had he found him less piously employed, for that has nothing to do with the play, but the tenor and tone of Hamlet's speech shows him glad to have an excuse not to kill him, an excuse which to Shakespeare's audience was quite colourable, and which we can believe or disbelieve to have been so to Hamlet himself, according to our tastes. That Hamlet is here taking cover behind an excuse is made the more likely because on the Ghost's reappearance he makes a frantic effort to transfer the burden of inaction from himself to his instigator, when he cries out,

> Do not look upon me
> Lest with this piteous action you convert
> My stern effects: then what I have to do
> Will want true colour; tears perchance for blood.

Hamlet knows that once already what he has to do has wanted true colour. As to the motives of Hamlet's gladness to have an excuse, we may conjecture to our hearts' content. It may be no more than that he was so absorbed in his resentment against his mother that the revenge of his father's death – an irreversible event – was a mere irrelevance, a matter of minor importance, to which his mind was never truly directed. No amount of vengeance on Claudius would alter the fact of his mother's defilement. And his mother must be dealt with directly. Hamlet with his clear intellect minded about the relevance of things. He was pleased enough to let Rosencrantz and Guildenstern die, for their crime had nothing to do with any overriding motive and its punishment he found to be apt. But I must mention Peter Alexander's sensitive and penetrating notion. This, occurring as it does in a book which, though admirable in content, makes the strategic error of uniting in one treatment the most severely factual with the delicately critical, is only too likely to be passed over. Alexander's treatment is too long to quote entire; and the following sentences must suffice:

Hamlet's purpose has been blunted by nothing more than the natural reluctance in a man of proved nerve, courage, and resolution, to stab a defenceless man. For this is his only resource. He cannot challenge the king; if the deed is to be done, it must be done in cold blood, in circumstances such as the prayer-scene does no more than set out in extreme form. And the more helpless the murderer the more reluctant the avenger. Hamlet's adversary must strike the first blow. Not that Hamlet can admit to himself, even for a moment, that this is what holds his hand. So unconscious is he of any virtue in this noble compunction that he cannot find words shameful enough to characterize it or blasphemous enough to excuse it.

Finally, it must be remembered that the notion of Hamlet's withholding his true motives for sparing Claudius had nothing originally to do with the new psychology but was formulated in the eighteenth century. Here is William Richardson's version of it from *Essays on Shakespeare's Dramatic Characters* (1784), p. 159. Speaking of Hamlet's expressed motives for sparing Claudius he says:

These are not his real sentiments. There is nothing in the whole character of Hamlet that justifies such savage enormity. . . . I would ask, then, whether, on many occasions, we do not alledge those considerations as the motives of our conduct, which really are not our motives? Nay, is not this sometimes done almost without our knowledge? Is it not done when we have no intention to deceive others; but when, by the influences of some present passion, we deceive ourselves? . . . Sense of supposed duty, and a regard to character, prompt him to slay his uncle; and he is with-held at that particular moment, by the ascendant of a gentle disposition; by the scruples, and perhaps weakness, of extreme sensibility. But how can he answer to the world, and to his sense of duty, for missing this opportunity? The real motive cannot be urged. Instead of excusing, it would expose him, he thinks, to censure; perhaps to contempt. He casts about for a motive; and one better suited to the opinions of the multitude, and better calculated to lull resentment, is immediately suggested. He indulges and shelters himself under the subterfuge. He alledges, as direct causes of his delay, motives that could never influence his conduct.

APPENDIX C

'This dull and long-continued truce'

Close study would reveal many ways in which Lydgate could explain difficulties of detail in *Troilus and Cressida*. Here is an example.

When in the play's third scene Aeneas arrives in the Greek council to bring the challenge he says that Hector complains of 'growing rusty in this dull and long-continued truce'. This flagrantly contradicts the previous scene, whose date in the play appears to be just before the council scene, where Pandarus hears the retreat sounded and comments on the Trojan leaders as they return from battle. Hector is among them, and Pandarus points out the hacks on his helmet. Now when Shakespeare mentioned the truce he was remembering Lydgate or Caxton and forgetting his own previous scene. There are several long truces in Lydgate. The first, of eight weeks, comes after the first general battle which ended with Hector's mistaken magnanimity in calling off the battle at Ajax's request. During this truce there is a Greek council, and Palamedes undermines Agamemnon's authority by complaining that his election as commander-in-chief was irregular. And he says he will not obey him. Now Shakespeare's council of Greeks, although Palamedes is not of it, concerns the questions of discipline and obedience like Lydgate's, and Shakespeare, thinking of their common theme, thinks also of the truce during which Lydgate's council occurs.

APPENDIX D

'This is, and is not, Cressid'

Observation of the kind of spiritual crisis noted in my text (p. 80) as common to Hamlet and Troilus will be but too apt to confirm the opinions of those who see in the two plays a reflection of Shakespeare's own experience at this time. Gertrude let Hamlet down, Cressida Troilus: therefore in these years someone let down Shakespeare. Although in these plays I cannot see any lack of dramatic aptness that might make us suspect a personal, non-dramatic, extrinsic emotion, I must note that this is precisely what I did find* in a different and unexpected context, the scene of *Henry V* where Henry confronts the conspirators. In Henry's words to Lord Scroop I found the same type of feeling, the bewilderment and incredulity of a trusting man who finds that he has been let down, expressed with an emotional sincerity not found elsewhere in the play and not at all apt to the character of the speaker. Here are the lines from the speech closest to the words of Troilus:

> Thou that didst bear the key of all my counsels,
> That knew'st the very bottom of my soul,
> That almost might'st have coin'd me into gold
> Wouldst thou have practis'd on me for thy use,
> May it be possible that foreign hire
> Could out of these extract one spark of evil
> That might annoy my finger? 'tis so strange
> That, though the truth of it stands off as gross
> As black and white, my eye will scarcely see it.

The idea is the same: this is and is not Scroop. Those who want to draw biographical conclusions from the idea will thus have to go back to *Henry V* at least, and will find that play a more likely field for conjecture than *Troilus and Cressida*.

* In my *Shakespeare's History Plays* (London, 1945, New York, 1946), p. 308.

APPENDIX E

Stratification in All's Well

A problem that must be posed, though it cannot be solved, is that of stratification. Are there or are there not relics of an earlier play incorporated in our text? That the text is bad, that there are gaps, and that, as Dover Wilson holds, there is evidence of a hasty copyist may be true; but these facts do not in themselves prove either different Shakespearean strata or the work of a collaborator. The hasty copyist could have worked on a number of scrappy sheets of Shakespeare's writing, all contemporary. Again the stage direction at II. 3. 190 'Parolles and Lafeu stay behind commenting on this wedding' does indeed look like an intrusion; and may well be a memorandum on the original manuscript referring to the actual composition of the play and wrongly perpetuated into a stage direction. But there is no need to think with Dover Wilson that it is Shakespeare's direction to his collaborator. Anyone who has written books will know the habit of jotting down in the manuscript itself a memorandum of what is to follow, lest interruption should produce oblivion and spoil the scheme. The stage direction may well be Shakespeare's memorandum at the end of a day's work, or at some other interruption, of how he intended to continue. Other explanations can be manufactured; and the plain truth is that there is no certainty.

I have dealt in the text with the authenticity of Parolles's conversation with Helena on virginity (I. 1. 117) and with the two long stretches of rhyme (II. 1. 133 and II. 3. 78). Other pieces of rhyming are less surprising and can be largely explained as an exaggeration of common practice; yet this exaggeration in conjunction with the more surprising uses must make us think. Here are the main instances. At the end of I. 1, when Parolles has left, Helena soliloquizes for fourteen lines, a large measure of couplets to give the common indication of finality. Moreover these couplets are like those in Act Two in that they promote action: in fact it is here that Helena first discloses her resolve to cure the King –

> The King's disease – my project may deceive me;
> But my intents are fixt and will not leave me.

In I. 3. 134, where the Folio gives Helena's entrance in response to the Countess's summons, the Countess soliloquizes on Helena's love-sick air in rhyme:

> Even so it was with me when I was young.
>   If ever we are nature's, these are ours: this thorn
> Doth to our rose of youth rightly belong;
>   Our blood to us, this to our blood is born.
> It is the show and seal of nature's truth,
>   Where love's strong passion is impress'd in youth.

Such rhyming may recall *Love's Labour's Lost*; but the Countess here indulges in personal reminiscence, and it is quite appropriate if she marks off the past by a formal and stylized kind of utterances. In II. 3, where Helena makes her choice in rhyme, the King, after chiding Bertram in blank verse, suddenly falls into couplets for a homily on honour depending on native virtue and not on titles, and then, after a few lines of blank verse, speaks five lines containing two internal rhymes (160–4):

>   ... that canst not *dream*
> We, poising us in her defective scale,
> Shall weigh thee to the *beam*; that wilt not *know*
> It is in us to plant thine honour where
> We please to have it *grow*.

Here the strata-hunters find powerful evidence. In the actual couplets, they think, Shakespeare borrowed from an old play and when he began again turning couplets into blank verse he gave himself away by admitting two rhymes which originally ended a pair of couplets. But, when examined, the evidence is not conclusive. The surprising thing is that Shakespeare used couplets at this place at all; and you in no wise explain this surprise by asserting that his couplets were borrowed. And granted that Shakespeare wanted couplets just there, there is not the slightest reason why he should not have written them then and there without recourse to an old play. And as for the internal rhyme, a cursory inspection of the first act of *Hamlet* has revealed three places where it occurs, one of them about the length of the passage in *All's Well* and containing one pair and one trio of internal rhymes:

> ... whose common theme
> Is death of fathers, and who still hath *cried*,
> From the first corse till he that *died* to-day,
> 'This must be *so*'. We pray you *throw* to earth
> This unprevailing *woe*.

To find in all the internal rhymes of Shakespeare evidence of 'fossil' couplets is patently absurd. And if this is a general rule, what justification is there for breaking it at convenience? Again, I am not saying that the notion that Shakespeare was using an old play can be disproved: I merely maintain that the notion is not necessary.

In III. 4 Helena's letter to the Countess, beginning 'I am St Jaques' pilgrim' is in rhyming quatrains. But a pilgrim has forsaken the norm of life and may fitly use an abnormal way of expression. Finally there are a few couplets in the last scene of the play. First, the King (v. 3. 61) speaks three rather flat couplets on Helena's supposed death; but he adds his own explanation of them by calling them 'Sweet Helen's knell', and they are not out of keeping with the other couplets of the play. Later Diana, speaking in riddles, just before the whole truth comes out, uses a few couplets; and riddles should of course be in rhyme. And Helena, after a few words of moving blank verse –

> No, my good lord,
> 'Tis but the shadow of a wife you see;
> The name and not the thing –

joins with Bertram to speak a few conventional couplets in final reconciliation. They are not in themselves surprising.

Shakespeare's use of the couplet, then, should make us think. But our thoughts need not demand as explanation the intrusion of earlier verse. Some of these couplets are doing much what his couplets usually do, others in their strangeness point to an unusual mood in him when he wrote the play.

INDEX

INDEX

READ MORE IN PENGUIN

In every corner of the world, on every subject under the sun, Penguin represents quality and variety – the very best in publishing today.

For complete information about books available from Penguin – including Puffins, Penguin Classics and Arkana – and how to order them, write to us at the appropriate address below. Please note that for copyright reasons the selection of books varies from country to country.

In the United Kingdom: Please write to *Dept. JC, Penguin Books Ltd, FREEPOST, West Drayton, Middlesex UB7 0BR*

If you have any difficulty in obtaining a title, please send your order with the correct money, plus ten per cent for postage and packaging, to *PO Box No. 11, West Drayton, Middlesex UB7 0BR*

In the United States: Please write to *Penguin USA Inc., 375 Hudson Street, New York, NY 10014*

In Canada: Please write to *Penguin Books Canada Ltd, 10 Alcorn Avenue, Suite 300, Toronto, Ontario M4V 3B2*

In Australia: Please write to *Penguin Books Australia Ltd, 487 Maroondah Highway, Ringwood, Victoria 3134*

In New Zealand: Please write to *Penguin Books (NZ) Ltd,182–190 Wairau Road, Private Bag, Takapuna, Auckland 9*

In India: Please write to *Penguin Books India Pvt Ltd, 706 Eros Apartments, 56 Nehru Place, New Delhi 110 019*

In the Netherlands: Please write to *Penguin Books Netherlands B.V., Keizersgracht 231 NL–1016 DV Amsterdam*

In Germany: Please write to *Penguin Books Deutschland GmbH, Friedrichstrasse 10–12, W–6000 Frankfurt/Main 1*

In Spain: Please write to *Penguin Books S. A., C. San Bernardo 117–6° E–28015 Madrid*

In Italy: Please write to *Penguin Italia s.r.l., Via Felice Casati 20, I–20124 Milano*

In France: Please write to *Penguin France S. A., 17 rue Lejeune, F–31000 Toulouse*

In Japan: Please write to *Penguin Books Japan, Ishikiribashi Building, 2–5–4, Suido, Tokyo 112*

In Greece: Please write to *Penguin Hellas Ltd, Dimocritou 3, GR–106 71 Athens*

In South Africa: Please write to *Longman Penguin Southern Africa (Pty) Ltd, Private Bag X08, Bertsham 2013*

READ MORE IN PENGUIN

THE NEW PENGUIN SHAKESPEARE

All's Well That Ends Well	Barbara Everett
Antony and Cleopatra	Emrys Jones
As You Like It	H. J. Oliver
The Comedy of Errors	Stanley Wells
Coriolanus	G. R. Hibbard
Hamlet	T. J. B. Spencer
Henry IV, Part 1	P. H. Davison
Henry IV, Part 2	P. H. Davison
Henry V	A. R. Humphreys
Henry VI, Part 1	Norman Sanders
Henry VI, Part 2	Norman Sanders
Henry VI, Part 3	Norman Sanders
Henry VIII	A. R. Humphreys
Julius Caesar	Norman Sanders
King John	R. L. Smallwood
King Lear	G. K. Hunter
Love's Labour's Lost	John Kerrigan
Macbeth	G. K. Hunter
Measure for Measure	J. M. Nosworthy
The Merchant of Venice	W. Moelwyn Merchant
The Merry Wives of Windsor	G. R. Hibbard
A Midsummer Night's Dream	Stanley Wells
Much Ado About Nothing	R. A. Foakes
The Narrative Poems	Maurice Evans
Othello	Kenneth Muir
Pericles	Philip Edwards
Richard II	Stanley Wells
Richard III	E. A. J. Honigmann
Romeo and Juliet	T. J. B. Spencer
The Sonnets and A Lover's Complaint	John Kerrigan
The Taming of the Shrew	G. R. Hibbard
The Tempest	Anne Barton
Timon of Athens	G. R. Hibbard
Troilus and Cressida	R. A. Foakes
Twelfth Night	M. M. Mahood
The Two Gentlemen of Verona	Norman Sanders
The Two Noble Kinsmen	N. W. Bawcutt
The Winter's Tale	Ernest Schanzer

READ MORE IN PENGUIN

LITERARY CRITICISM

The English Novel Walter Allen

In this 'refreshingly alert' (*The Times Literary Supplement*) landmark panorama of English fiction, the development of the novel is traced from *The Pilgrim's Progress* to Joyce and Lawrence.

Sexual Personae Camille Paglia

'A powerful book ... interprets western culture as a sexual battleground pitting the Apollonian desire for order against the forces of Dionysian darkness' – *The Times*

The Anatomy of Criticism Northrop Frye

'Here is a book fundamental enough to be entitled *Principia Critica*,' wrote one critic. Northrop Frye's seminal masterpiece was the first work to argue for the status of literary criticism as a science: a true discipline whose techniques and approaches could systematically – and beneficially – be evaluated, quantified and categorized.

Art and Literature Sigmund Freud

Volume 15 of the Penguin Freud Library contains various writings that Freud intended mainly for the non-specialist reader. They include such topics as the theory of instincts, libido and repression, infantile sexuality, Oedipus complex, the sexual factor in neurosis and much more.

Modernism Malcolm Bradbury and James McFarlane (eds.)

'The Modern movement in the arts transformed consciousness and artistic form just as the energies of modernity transformed forever the nature, the speed, the sensation of human life' write the editors in their new Preface. This now classic survey explores the ideas, the groupings and the social tensions that shaped this transformation, as well as the literature itself.

READ MORE IN PENGUIN

LITERARY CRITICISM

A Lover's Discourse Roland Barthes

'*A Lover's Discourse* ... may be the most detailed, painstaking anatomy of desire we are ever likely to see or need again ... The book is an ecstatic celebration of love and language and ... readers interested in either or both ... will enjoy savouring its rich and dark delights' – *Washington Post Book World*

The New Pelican Guide to English Literature Boris Ford (ed.)

The indispensable critical guide to English and American literature in nine volumes, erudite yet accessible. From the ages of Chaucer and Shakespeare, via Georgian satirists and Victorian social critics, to the leading writers of the 1980s, all literary life is here.

The Theatre of the Absurd Martin Esslin

This classic study of the dramatists of the Absurd examines the origins, nature and future of a movement whose significance has transcended the bounds of the stage and influenced the whole intellectual climate of our time.

Introducing Shakespeare G. B. Harrison

An excellent popular introduction to Shakespeare – the legend, the (tantalizingly ill-recorded) life and the work – in the context of his times: theatrical rivalry, literary piracy, the famous performance of Richard II in support of Essex, and the fire which finally destroyed the Globe.

Aspects of the Novel E. M. Forster

'I say that I have never met this kind of perspicacity in literary criticism before. I could quote scores of examples of startling excellence' – Arnold Bennett. Originating in a course of lectures given at Cambridge, *Aspects of the Novel* is full of E. M. Forster's habitual wit, wisdom and freshness of approach.